P9-ARU-814

A CONSERVATIVE INTRODUCTION TO THE NEW TESTAMENT

A Conservative Introduction to the New Testament

By

Samuel A. Cartledge, A.M., B.D., Ph.D.,
Professor of New Testament Literature and Exegesis,
Columbia Theological Seminary,
Decatur, Georgia

Third Edition

ZONDERVAN PUBLISHING HOUSE
Grand Rapids Michigan

First Edition, 1938
Second Edition, 1939
Third Edition, 1941

EIGHT-FIFTEEN FRANKLIN STREET
GRAND RAPIDS, MICHIGAN

TO
M. G. K. C.

PREFACE

THE purpose of this *Introduction* is to make it possible for the student of the Bible to read and study his New Testament more intelligently. It attempts to show how this wonderful ancient, Oriental book may be made a book of vital importance for the twentieth-century reader. It attempts to give the answers to many of the questions that naturally present themselves to thoughtful readers of the New Testament.

An attempt has been made to steer a middle course in the presentation of the material at hand. The author does not simply present the conclusions which he has reached, but he seeks to give the evidence and the reasoning by which those conclusions were reached. At times the reader must draw his own conclusions from the evidence presented when no conclusions are presented; at all times the reader should reach his own conclusions from the evidence, whether they agree with those of the author or not. This *Introduction* seeks to present all of the more important facts and theories in the field at present. It does not attempt to present all of the minor theories. Nor does it attempt to list all of the scholars who hold the various views presented. It does not seek to take the place of the more exhaustive treatments, such as those of Moffat and Zahn.

Accuracy has been striven for, but technicalities have been avoided wherever possible. It is hoped that this book may prove useful to the average minister or thoughtful student of the New Testament. It will probably lend itself to use in the average college course in New Testament or a seminary course in New Testament introduction; it would serve as a summary treatment for the more detailed courses in the field. If it is used in leadership training classes, the teacher should select those parts that the time at hand and the preparation of the students may allow; other parts may be used as parallel reading

This *Introduction* is written from the Conservative point of view. Distinctive features of Conservatism are a belief in the deity of Jesus, in the miraculous, and in the inspiration of the Scriptures. The author is well aware that there are others who differ quite widely from this viewpoint. New Testament scholars may differ in their theories but they should not differ when dealing with facts. Many of the theories, even, are held in common by scholars of all schools of interpretation. The author seeks at all times to be fair, even with those with whom he must differ. An intelligent Conservative should know his own side and be able to give reasons for his faith; he should know, also, something of the views of other sides, so that he may be a Conservative from choice, not from ignorance.

The author owes much to others who have written in this field; also to those who have been kind enough to read the manuscript and offer helpful suggestions. The author alone is, of course, responsible for the imperfections that remain.

PREFACE TO THE SECOND EDITION

As the second edition is following so soon after the first, it has seemed wise to make no changes in the text of the book. Some footnotes have been added, mainly to take account of some of the most recent literature in the field. Larger type has been used, so the page numbers will be different from the first edition.

Some few have suggested that the use of the word "Conservative" in the title of the book implied that the author approached the subject with a closed mind. Such was not the intention of the word. After weighing the evidence as fairly as he could, the author has reached Conservative conclusions; he believes that these conclusions are in thorough harmony with the positions of historic Christianity and also with the facts of historical criticism.

S. A. C.

Columbia Theological Seminary,
Decatur, Georgia

CONTENTS

PART ONE, GENERAL INTRODUCTION

PART TWO, SPECIAL INTRODUCTION

APPENDIX

PART ONE
GENERAL INTRODUCTION

I

PRINCIPLES OF INTERPRETATION

The Bible has for centuries been the most important book known to mankind. It has been the source of life and light for untold millions. It has brought to men the highest conception of religion that has ever been known. Rightly we treasure it today as we treasure no other book. Rightly ministers use it as the primary source of their preaching. Rightly all Christians seek to find the meaning of God's revelation for their lives.

The Bible would speak to us. We should hear and understand. When we have understood, then we may live in accordance with God's will for us.

The providence of God and the heroism of our fathers have preserved the Bible for us today. All of us have access to it in our own language; some of us, in the original languages. Some of it is so plain that it may be understood by the smallest child; some of it is too deep for the wisest men. Most of it can be understood by those who are willing to pay the price for true interpretation.

Men down through the centuries have given their lives to the study of the Bible. Some of their work has been of little or no value, but much of it has been most valuable. Out of this accumulated study, there have come principles of interpretation and much material to use in putting these principles in practice.

Every serious student of the Bible should know something of these principles and have access to at least the more important parts of the material produced by the Biblical scholars.

In general, the principles for interpretation of the Bible are the same as those for interpreting any book. Many of them we use daily, unconsciously. But as the Bible is an ancient book, an Oriental book, and such an important book, we should be most careful to interpret it aright. We must not read into the Bible our own notions or pet ideas, but must let it speak its own truth to us. The fact that so many different interpretations have been put on various parts of the Bible has made many feel that there cannot be any accurate, trustworthy interpretation. But there may be. The false interpretations should make us want more than ever to find the true ones. Jesus said, "Ye shall know the truth, and the truth shall make you free."

The basic principle of interpretation is that every writing must be interpreted in the light of its context. The original context gave the writing its meaning, and if the context is completely restored the original meaning will be revealed. The restoration of the complete context is an ideal which it is usually impossible to attain; but the interpreter must try to restore it as fully as possible, knowing that the closer he comes to the ideal of complete restoration the more certain he can be about the correctness of his interpretation. Where important parts of the context cannot be restored by facts, they must be restored by theory. That is one reason why interpretations differ at times; different interpreters use different theories.

We must realize the wealth of meaning in the term "context." All scholars today agree that we must use grammatico-historical interpretation; that is, that we must strive to reconstruct completely the grammatical and historical contexts. Those are two basic elements in the context, but it may be useful to add also the literary, logical, and psychological contexts.

The New Testament was written in Greek. In trying to reach a complete interpretation of a certain passage, it will be necessary to go to that passage in the original language and get all the light that can be thrown on it by the words used in the passage and the other passages related to it. The Greek of the first century will throw most light on New Testament passages, but light may be thrown by the Greek of any period or by other related languages. A student who can approach interpretation only through a translation must work under a handicap, because no translation can bring out completely the meaning and force of the original. All scholars realize the importance of the scientific study of the original language of the work to be interpreted. We know much about the Greek language today, but there is much still to be learned. There are excellent translations available for the student who cannot go to the original. In any language, though, we must deal fairly with the language.

The different New Testament books were written in various historical backgrounds. They were written in the light of these backgrounds. They were written for the purpose of meeting definite historical situations. We must seek to reconstruct as completely as possible this historical background and see what light it has to throw on the passage to be interpreted. Grave errors in interpretation have been made by neglecting this principle. A command that would be valid under certain circumstances would be entirely meaningless under other circumstances. A knowledge of some of the history of Corinth helps us understand why Paul told the women of that city to wear their veils to church; of the Galatians, why he told them that they must not be circumcised. The more we can know about the historical circumstances that called forth the New Testament books the more certain can our interpretation of them be. We welcome all the light that history can give us. We are all seeking more light.

We must also understand the literary context. What literary form is used in the passage under consideration? What is the meaning of that form? Poetry must not be interpreted as prose. Parables and allegories and the various figures of speech must be handled correctly. At times this part of the context is easy to handle; at times, extremely difficult. Its neglect has often led to the most fantastic interpretations.

The passage for interpretation will be a part of a larger unit. What is the logical train of thought in which the passage occurs? How does the passage fit into the larger whole? The logic of the whole passage will frequently determine the meaning of a part of the passage.

The passage was written by a certain human author to certain other human beings. We must try to understand the workings of the minds of the author and those to whom he wrote. We must remember that they were first-century peoples, most of them Orientals. We must try to understand the workings of a first-century Oriental mind. We must also remember the individual differences. In interpreting a part of a Pauline epistle, we must look for all the light we can get from a knowledge of the mind of Paul; we must also try to determine what effect he was trying to produce on the minds of his original readers.

All of these principles must be carefully used in seeking to determine what the original writer wanted the original reader to get from his writing. That must come first. Then we should seek to determine the meaning of the writing for ourselves. Often that is very easy; at times it is not. We must distinguish between the eternal principles underlying a passage and the application of those principles to temporary circumstances. In America, for example, we no longer have to worry with the problem of eating meat offered to idols, but underneath that rather strange chapter of First Corinthians we see great eternal truths, especially that each of us has some influence and has the duty to use that influence to build up rather than to tear down others. The great principles do not change, but their application may change as the circumstances change. The Bible is an old book, but it is also a very modern book; its truths are of vital importance to every age. We must make them our own.

II

THE TRANSMISSION OF THE GREEK TEXT

THE writers of the books of the New Testament did not have the advantages of the printing press by which thousands of identical copies of their books could be scattered abroad and preserved for future ages. These writers, or their scribes, wrote with pen and ink on papyrus rolls[1] normally, making, of course, only one copy at a time. When other copies were desired for circulation, they too had to be copied off by hand. Papyrus becomes brittle with age, so it was not long before the original manuscripts of the various books of the New Testament were all worn out. The very oldest manuscripts that are in existence today are copies of copies of the originals, with a period of about two hundred years between the originals and the oldest manuscript of any length. Anyone who has tried to do any copy work himself knows that it is impossible to copy any long work without making some more or less important mistakes. So it was in the case of the manuscripts of the New Testament; of the many thousands that we have today, no two are just alike. How may we determine what the original text was? Can we do it? Those who feel that the Bible is the most im-

[1] The use by Christians of the codex, or book, form has been traced to the early part of the second century. It may be that some of the New Testament books were written first in these codices.

portant book ever written have an ardent desire to get as close as possible to the very words of the inspired writers. In trying to recover the best possible text, scholars have developed the science of textual criticism. The Christian Church owes a great debt of gratitude to those scholars who have given their lives that we might have a Greek text today that can be considered such an accurate reproduction of the text of the inspired writers.

At first thought, the task of New Testament textual criticism seems a hopeless one. Yet let us notice what a favorable position is occupied by the New Testament in comparison with other authors of antiquity. The New Testament writings are separated from their earliest manuscript by about 200 years. Virgil is next with an interval of about 350 years; Livy has 500 years; Terence, 700; Horace, 900; Demosthenes, 1200; Plato, 1300; while the great Greek dramatists have an interval of 1400 years or more. Then again, consider the number of extant manuscripts. There is only one extant copy of the Greek Anthology; the plays of Aeschylus survive in only fifty manuscripts, none of which is complete; those of Sophocles, in about a hundred; Euripides, Cicero, Virgil, and some of the others have several hundred. But when we come to the New Testament, we find 4000 extant manuscripts of all or parts of it in the Greek, to say nothing of 10,000 copies of a translation of it into Latin and numerous manuscripts of translations into other languages. We feel that we have substantially accurate copies of the great Classical authors; should we not even more in the case of the New Testament, when we have so many more manuscripts written so much closer to the time of the original writings? The greatest of the modern textual critics, Westcott and Hort, have this to say about the present accuracy of the New Testament text:[2] "The proportion of words virtually accepted on all hands as raised above doubt is very great, not less, on a rough computation, than seven-eighths of the whole. The remaining eighth, therefore, formed in great part by changes of order and other comparative trivialities, constitute the whole area of criticism. If the principles followed in this edition are sound, this area may be very greatly reduced. Recognizing to the full the duty of abstinence from peremptory decision in cases where the evidence leaves the judgment in suspense between two or more readings, we find that, setting aside differences of orthography, the words in our opinion still subject to doubt only make up about one-sixtieth of the whole New Testament. In this second estimate the proportion of comparatively trivial variations is beyond measure larger than in the former; so that the amount of what can in any sense be called substantial variation is but a small residuary variation, and can hardly form more than a thousandth part of the entire text." Kenyon assures us that no single doctrine of Christianity rests upon a disputed text. Textual critics have done wonderful work in reducing the doubtful area from one-eighth to one-thousandth. They are still at work. Let us see something of their methods and the materials with which they work.

The Greek Manuscripts

The most valuable materials for the reconstruction of the best possible Greek text are, of course, the Greek manuscripts. These manuscripts are of two kinds, the uncials and the cursives. The uncial manuscripts are those written entirely in capital letters. This form of writing was employed in writing our New Testament

[2] The New Testament in the Original Greek, vol. II, p. 2.

manuscripts from the earliest that we have until the tenth century. Beginning with the ninth century, an easier and quicker method of writing began to be employed, the cursive or running hand, in which the small letters of the alphabet were used; and they were joined together so that the scribe could make several letters without removing the pen from the manuscript. The uncial manuscripts did not leave space between words, while the cursives did leave such space with a fair degree of regularity; modern editors are free to divide the letters into words as they think best. Our earliest manuscripts were not written with punctuation or with the Greek accents or breathings; later, scribes began to put these in, little by little, as seemed best to them; here again modern scholars and editors must use their own judgment about these rather minor matters. Verse and chapter divisions, as we now know them, are extremely modern inventions and have no place in a consideration of the manuscripts. Our earliest manuscripts were written on papyrus, probably in the roll form, but only a few Biblical papyri are known now. Most of our manuscripts were written on parchment in the codex, or book, form. Some of the manuscripts from the fourteenth century on are written on paper. Printing was invented in the latter part of the fifteenth century, so we have few manuscripts after that time. Let us consider some of the more important individual manuscripts, taking them in the order in which they became known to the textual critics.

The Codex Bezae, whose symbol is "D," contains the Bible written in both Greek and Latin, the former on the left-hand page and the latter on the right. It is a sixth century uncial, containing, in the New Testament section, the gospels, in the order, Matthew, John, Luke, and Mark, the Acts, and a Latin fragment of III John. It is our chief manuscript of the "Western" type of text, which, as we shall see, is a very peculiar and erratic type. This manuscript contains a number of additions to what we consider the true text, some of which later found their way into the text used by our English King James translators, such as the story of the woman taken in adultery in John 8. Stephanus, in his 1500 edition of the Greek Testament, had some notes taken from a collation of this manuscript. Theodore Beza obtained the manuscript from a monastery in Lyons in 1562, used it slightly in some of the later editions of his Greek Testament, and then presented it to the University of Cambridge, in whose keeping it still remains.

Codex Alexandrinus, or "A," is a fifth century manuscript of the Bible, including, in addition, an almost complete copy of the letters of Clement. All of the books of the New Testament are included, though there are gaps in Matthew, John, and II Corinthians. In the gospels this manuscript gives us the rather poor "Syrian" type of text, but in the other books it is one of the primary witnesses for the purest type of text, the "Neutral." Alexandrinus was brought to Constantinople in 1621 by the Patriarch Cyral Lucar when he transferred to that city from Alexandria. Lucar offered the manuscript to King James I of England; James died before it came, so it was received by Charles I in 1627. It is now in the British Museum.

Codex Ephraemi Rescriptus, or "C," is also a fifth century uncial. This manuscript is *palimpsest*; that is, the original New Testament writing was more or less completely erased or washed from the parchment and then the writings of St. Ephraem of Syria were written in. The manuscript once contained the whole Bible, but now we have only fragments of it left. It is one of the primary witnesses for the Neutral type of text. The under writing can be recovered fairly well, especially by using modern chemistry and photography. Wetstein made a collation of it in 1716 for Bentley. Tischendorf published a complete edition of the New Testament parts in 1843 and the Old in 1845. The manuscript was for a time in the hands of the Medici family; Catherine took it to Paris, where it came to the library which is now known as the Bibliotheque Nationale.

Codex Vaticanus, "B," is our most important manuscript presenting the Neutral type of text. It is a fourth century manuscript of the Bible; it lacks the last few chapters of Hebrews, the Pastoral Epistles, and Revelation. It has been in the Vatican Library at Rome since 1481, at least. One of the Vatican librarians made a collation of it, but it was not used until 1819. The manuscript was brought by Napoleon to Paris, where the scholar Hug identified it and called the attention of scholars to it. After the downfall of Napoleon, it was returned to the Vatican. Several more poor collations of the manuscript were made, but competent text critics were not able to obtain permission to do careful work on it. Several more or less accurate printed reproductions of it were made before it was finally made completely and accurately known to scholars through a photographic facsimile edition in 1890.

Codex Sinaiticus, or Aleph (the first letter in the Hebrew alphabet), is a fourth century manuscript of the Bible, containing the whole of the New Testament and the Epistle of Barnabas and the Shepherd of Hermas. The account of its discovery by the great German textual critic Tischendorf is one of the most interesting chapters of textual history. While visiting in the monastery of St. Catherine on Mount Sinai, he noticed in the waste basket some parchment leaves that were being used to light the lamps. He was allowed to take this waste paper, which proved to be forty-three leaves from various parts of the Greek Old Testament. He was shown other sections of the Old Testament, but he was not allowed to have them. In 1853, nine years later, he made a second trip to the monastery but found nothing. In 1859, however, on his third trip, he found not only other parts of the Old Testament, but also the complete New Testament. He was finally able to persuade the monastery authorities to present the manuscript to the Czar, the great patron of the Greek Catholic Church, who placed it in the Imperial Library in St. Petersburg, where it remained until 1933, when it was purchased by the British museum for the huge sum of a hundred thousand pounds. Tischendorf issued an edition printed in facsimile type in 1862, and a photographic facsimile edition was published in 1911 by the Oxford University Press. The value of this great manuscript is second only to Codex Vaticanus, as it, too, is a leading witness to the Neutral type of text.

The Freer Gospels, or Codex Washingtoniensis, or "W," is a Gospels manuscript of the fifth or even fourth century. Mr. C. L. Freer of Detroit bought this manuscript from a dealer near Cairo in 1906. A representative of the British Museum had seen the manuscript before this and had returned to England to arrange for the purchase of it, but Mr. Freer came along with the money just in time to purchase this treasure and send it to America. Mr. Freer was not a textual scholar himself, so he sent the manuscript to the University of Michigan. There Professor Sanders and his associates made a careful study of it. Photographic facsimile editions of the Gospels and certain books of the Old Testament have been published. The manuscript is now in the Freer Art Gallery in Washington. "W" does not have the same type of text throughout;

in fact, all the major types of text are found in it. An unusual ending for the gospel of Mark has been found only in "W." It is our second great Greek uncial that has parts of the gospels in the Western type of text.

Codex Koridethi, or Theta (the Greek "th"), was brought to the attention of the scholarly world by von Soden, whose massive edition of the Greek Testament was completed in 1913. This manuscript of the Gospels was produced by a scribe who drew, rather than wrote, his letters, so it is impossible to date it accurately; it may be about the seventh century. The type of text is an interesting mixture of Western and Neutral, which scholars have called "Caesarean," and which is proving one of the most interesting of the recent problems in the field of textual criticism. Dr. Nestle says that the manuscript is now in Leningrad.

In 1931 a most interesting manuscript discovery was announced by Mr. Chester Beatty of England. He had bought twelve papyrus manuscripts from dealers in Egypt; three of them were manuscripts of the New Testament; eight, of the Old Testament; and one, of the Book of Enoch. They range in date between the second and fifth centuries, so they are extremely early. The three New Testament manuscripts probably come from the third century, so they become our earliest direct evidence of the Greek text of substantial length. The first manuscript, P^{45}, consists of thirty leaves (sixty pages) from the gospels and Acts, all of them somewhat mutilated. Its text agrees closely with the great early families of the Westcott-Hort theory, especially the Neutral. In Mark, especially, however, its text is much like that mixture of the Neutral and Western, which may be a new text, the Caesarean. It probably comes from the first half of the third century, so it is a century older than the great uncials B and Aleph. The second manuscript, P^{46}, consists of eighty-six leaves of the Pauline Epistles. It probably comes from early in the third century. Its text is not Syrian in the least, and is far closer to the Neutral than to the Western. The third, P^{47}, is probably a late third-century manuscript, containing ten leaves of Revelation; it is most closely related to the primary uncials Aleph, A, and C.

Very recently a tiny fragment of the gospel of John, written on papyrus, was discovered in the John Rylands Library in England. It has been dated with some degree of certainty at about 125, which is by far the oldest New Testament manuscript. As it contains only parts of John 18: 31-33, 37, and 38, it is too short to give much textual help.

These are some of the most important of the Greek uncial manuscripts. There are about sixty of these that contain substantial portions of the New Testament and a hundred more containing smaller parts. There are well over two thousand of the Greek cursive manuscripts. Most of the cursives contain the poorest type of text, the Syrian, so they are not so valuable. The best of the known cursives is "33," which has a Neutral text that ranks with the best uncials. There are so many of the cursives that there are still hundreds of them yet to be worked by the textual critics.

The Greek manuscripts that have been considered so far are those that contain the continuous text of all or sections of the New Testament. Besides these, there are over fifteen hundred lectionaries, which give readings for the different days of the Church year, selections being taken from the gospels or epistles. Few lectionaries are earlier than the ninth century, so they have been considered of little importance. However, the value of the text varies in the different sections, and scholars are beginning to study these once neglected lesson books more carefully, hoping that new light may be thrown on at least the transmission of the text through the Middle Ages.[3]

Manuscripts in Other Languages

Very early, translations were made from the original Greek into many other languages, and the textual scholar must consider these too among his sources. Of course, a translation can never fully reproduce the original, so at times the versions can give no help about certain matters, such as the order of the words, of the presence or absence of the article. Then at times the manuscripts of even an early version may be late themselves, so that it becomes necessary to apply the principles of textual criticism to those manuscripts to obtain an accurate reproduction of the early text. In spite of these limitations, the versions can give us some really valuable evidence as to the locations and dates of the various textual families.

One of the Egyptian versions, the Bohairic, probably goes back to the second century and gives a very good presentation of the Neutral type of text. The other Egyptian version, the Sahidic, is probably not quite so early,[4] and while its text is primarily Neutral it has a rather large Western element.

The Old Latin version comes from the middle of the second century and is one of our primary witnesses of the Western type of text. Toward the end of the fourth century, the scholar Jerome made a new translation into Latin which became known as the Vulgate and which became the authoritative Bible of the Roman Catholic Church. There are something like ten thousand Vulgate manuscripts, so the textual criticism of the Vulgate is a tremendous, and largely unworked field.

---

[3] Cf. Studies in the Lectionary Text, vol. I, Colwell and Riddle, editors, 1933, University of Chicago Press.

[4] Though Lake and Kenyon would reverse the order.

The text of the Vulgate is not especially valuable, however, as it contains a large element of the Syrian text with just a little of the Western.

The older Syriac versions, the Sinaitic and Curetonian, go back to about 200 A.D.; they are important witnesses for the Western text. The common Syriac version, the Peshitto, from the fifth century, probably, and the other Syriac versions after it, all belong to the Syrian textual family.

There are many other versions, but they are later than these, and most of them give the traditional Syrian type of text.

The Writings of the Fathers

The early Church Fathers frequently made quotations from the New Testament in their writings, so that these writings must also be considered sources for textual work. Of course, there is the problem of getting the correct text of these writings, just as there was in the case of the versions. Then at times we cannot be sure whether the Father is quoting exactly or whether he is giving simply the sense of the passage, possibly from memory. Yet the fact that their writings go back so early and can be so definitely dated and placed, makes the testimony of the Fathers quite valuable. Origen's quotations at times come from the Neutral text and at times from the Western. Clement, Athanasius, and Cyril help us reconstruct the Neutral text. Tertullian, Irenaeus, and Cyprian quote largely from the Western text. Most of the other Fathers use the Syrian type.

The Westcott-Hort Theory

We have reviewed briefly the materials at the disposal of the textual critics. How are these materials used? The two great textual scholars, Drs. Westcott and

Hort, in preparing their critical edition of the Greek New Testament, which was published in 1881, developed a theory of textual criticism which took account of all the textual work done before their day, and which continues to be valid in all essentials in the light of textual study since that time. Let us get a brief survey of this theory.

I. *Internal Evidence of Readings:* All of our sources will agree as to the vast majority of the words, so that those words may be assumed to have come to us accurately from the original writings. But our sources disagree among themselves about a large number of the words, and it is our duty to decide which of the several possible variants is the correct one for each of the doubtful readings. The first bit of evidence which we are to use in determining which of the variants is the correct one is what Westcott and Hort call "internal evidence of readings." This evidence is of two kinds, "intrinsic" and "transcriptional." In using the intrinsic evidence, we seek to determine which of the variants in a particular case seems to present the reading that the author probably wrote. For example, one of the variants may make no sense whatever, so that we may assume that that variant was simply the result of a scribal blunder and not the original. When we have made a careful study of the style and thought of the author, we are in a position to determine rather accurately what he must have written in a large number of cases where there are variant readings.

When the intrinsic evidence leaves us still in doubt, we are to try next the transcriptional evidence. Scholars who have done much work with manuscripts are in a position to tell us the kinds of errors that the scribes frequently made. Let us try, then, all of our variants in a particular case, one by one, as the original, and see which one taken as the original best explains the other variants as scribal errors. For example, some manuscripts contain John 3: 16 and some do not; did the original manuscript have it? If we assume that the original did not have it, we must assume that some scribe inserted it, having invented it himself or having taken it from some other source—a possible but not probable explanation. If, however, we assume that the original contained the verse, we can readily see how some scribes may have accidentally omitted it from their manuscripts. The last few words of verse 15 are identical with those of verse 16; after the scribe had read those last words of 15 his eye went over to the manuscript which he was writing; when he had written those words, his eyes went back to the manuscript from which he was copying and fell, instead of on those words at the end of 15, on the same words at the end of 16; he thought that he had written those, so he started writing again at verse 17, and 16 was omitted entirely. That error of *homoioteleuton,* ("like-ending") is a very common one with scribes, so that we may be rather certain that the true variant is the one containing the verse. Most of the errors made by scribes are unintentional, such as *homoioteleuton,* mistaking similar letters, misunderstanding abbreviations, failing to remember correctly, failing to understand words when they are dictated, letting the pen slip a bit, or not knowing what to do with words found in the margin, whether to consider them words of explanation or words accidentally omitted by the former scribe. In a few cases we can see that scribes make intentional changes in the text, trying to improve the grammar or style, or trying to clear up some historical or doctrinal difficulty.

II. *Internal Evidence of Documents*: After we have applied the two kinds of internal evidence of readings to a large number of doubtful readings in a large number of manuscripts, we come to observe that a certain manuscript nearly always contains the reading that our evidence shows to have been the best one, while another manuscript is nearly always to be found on the side of the poorest reading; we come, then, to consider the former manuscript a far more valuable witness to the true text than the latter. Manuscripts can thus be ranked. Then when our internal evidence of readings fails to determine which variant is the best one, we will take the reading which is found in the best manuscripts, and that will probably be the original one.

III. *Genealogical Evidence*: In dealing with thousands of manuscripts, it is well-nigh impossible to rank them all accurately as suggested in the former paragraph. It is also impossible to present all the evidence of the manuscripts for all the variants in any usable form. It is possible to group our manuscripts after the fashion of a family tree on the principle that identity of reading implies identity of origin. This grouping must be done only after a long and careful study. Westcott and Hort have made such groups, and the evidence which they have presented in favor of their grouping has appealed to scholars as valid. This evidence occupies most of Volume II of their Greek Testament, so it will be impossible to present it here. Their grouping is as follows.

Certain manuscripts agree among themselves in presenting a type of text that they call the "Neutral" text. When this type of text is tested by the internal evidence, it is seen that it is the closest of all the types to the originals. The fact that some of the second century Fathers use this type of text shows us that it goes back at least into the second century. The manuscripts that belong to this family are B, Aleph, P^{45}, T in Luke and John, Xi in Luke, L, 33, Delta in Mark, C, Z in Matthew, R in Luke, Q, and P. (This is the grouping for the gospels; it is slightly different for other parts of the New Testament.) The Egyptian versions, especially the Bohairic, give us help in reconstructing this type of text, as do the Fathers Athanasius and Cyril and sometimes Origen.

At times, the Neutral manuscripts disagree among themselves and present two variants, one of which appears to be the original and one attempts to improve the grammar or style of the original. Westcott and Hort give the name "Alexandrian" to this artificially polished type of text. This type is almost never found in B, but it is found at times in all the other manuscripts that are regularly Neutral.

The third textual family is the "Western." It can be traced back to the second century too, but internal evidence is against considering it a good reproduction of the originals. The Western text is the careless type of text. It is characterized especially by paraphrase and interpolation. It is quite common to have genitive pronouns, objects, and conjunctions inserted. Sentences and even paragraphs are frequently inserted. The chief gospels witnesses for the Western text are: D, W in Mark 1-5, the Old Latin and the Old Syriac versions, Tertullian, Irenaeus, Clement of Alexandria, Cyprian, and sometimes Origen and Augustine. In the Epistles, E, F, and G join this group.

The last of the families is the "Syrian." Westcott and Hort give strong evidence for believing that this type of text resulted from a determined revision of the text and is the latest of the textual families. Probably in the fourth century some scholar or scholars determined to produce a text that would harmonize the differences between the three types of text that were then in existence. The principles used by these early textual critics were far from scientific, and so their text was a poor one; however, it was not long before the Syrian text became the popular and almost universal text. The evidence for the Syrian text includes practically everything that has not been given for the Neutral and Western; practically all of the cursive manuscripts belong here.

The true reading, then, is normally the Neutral one. However, we should always test even the Neutral reading very carefully by internal evidence before we consider the matter settled. In just a few places, Westcott and Hort think that the internal evidence proves that the Western text is right in leaving out some words that have been interpolated into the Neutral text. In a very few places, there is evidence suggesting that there may have been a primitive error made earlier than all of our known families, but Westcott and Hort would not put any reading into their text that could not be found in the extant manuscripts. In some places, it is impossible to determine which is the correct variant even after we have used all the evidence available; we have already noticed that Westcott and Hort say that only one word out of a thousand of any importance can be considered still in doubt after these principles of textual criticism have been applied.

After the Invention of Printing

Printing was first used in Europe about 1450, so after that time not many more manuscripts were produced. Thousands of textually identical copies could be produced, so the only variations were those between different editions.

It was some years before work was started on a printed Greek Testament. In 1502 the Catholic Cardinal Ximenes started work on a polyglot Bible, including, of course, the Greek New Testament. The New Testament volume was completed in 1514, but it was not actually published until 1522. The text was made from some of the manuscripts from the Vatican Library, but there is no trace of the use of the great Vatican manuscript, B. When this Complutensian Polyglot was completed, it was such a big, expensive work that it was never widely used.

While the Complutensian was in process of publication, a printer of Basle by the name of Froben decided that he wanted to be the first to print a Greek Testament. So he told one of the foremost scholars of the time, Erasmus, to get busy in a hurry and get him a text for printing. In less than a year Erasmus had produced his Greek text, a Latin translation of it, and explanatory notes; and this first Erasmus edition was printed in 1516. It did become the first Greek Testament, and it practically determined the text for all the Greek Testaments printed for more than three hundred years after it. In the production of his text, Erasmus used only five cursive manuscripts. In the gospels, he used two cursives, 1 of the eleventh century and 2 of the fifteenth century. For the Acts and epistles, he used the two cursives 2^{ap} of the thirteenth-fourteenth century and 4^{ap} of the fifteenth century. For Revelation, he had only the one cursive, 1^{r} of the twelfth century; this manuscript lacked the last six verses of the book, so Erasmus had to make his own ending by translating from the Latin. Naturally, a work produced so quickly, from so few and such late manuscripts, cannot compare in accuracy with the great modern printed editions; it was good for its day, but we can do far better now. There were four later Erasmus editions, in 1519, 1522, 1527, and 1535, into which a few changes were introduced from a few more manuscripts and the Complutensian Polyglot; but the text was really set in all essentials by the 1516 edition.

Robert Estienne (or Stephanus), a printer of Paris produced several very popular editions with texts almost identical with those of Erasmus between 1546 and 1551. The Western uncial D was used just a little. The 1551 edition was the first to divide the texts into verses, a great mechanical convenience.

Theodore Beza, who owned the great manuscripts D and D^2, produced nine editions between 1565 and 1604, all of which had substantially the Erasmus text.

The Elzevirs, printers of Leyden and Amsterdam, produced seven editions between 1624 and 1678, using almost exactly the Beza text. In their second edition, 1633, they used the words: "You have, now therefore, the text received by all"; thus this Erasmus-Stephanus-Beza-Elzevir text got the name of "Received Text," or "Textus Receptus." This advertisement carried no ecclesiastical authority of any kind back of it, but it did state a fact. The Received Text became the standard text for a long time; so highly did it become revered that scholars who attempted to produce a better text met the most intense opposition. It was the text which was used by the English King James translators.

By the eighteenth century, scholars had become quite dissatisfied with the old Received Text and wanted a better one. Many more manuscripts had come to light and had been worked. But the esteem of the Received Text was too much. Throughout the eighteenth century the Received Text was still printed, but many new readings began to be printed in the margins, and scholars began to work out principles of scientific textual criticism. The great names in this period include John Mill, Richard Bentley, John Albert Bengel, J. J. Wettstein, and J. J. Griesbach.

Finally, in the middle of the nineteenth century, we have the first printing of a new, critical Greek Testament. This honor belongs to Carl Lachmann, who produced several editions, the most important being the one of 1842-50. He followed the great uncials A, B, and C and Origen most closely. He did some grouping into families.

G. F. C. Tischendorf was a great discoverer, collator, and publisher of manuscripts; his greatest find was the splendid uncial Aleph, or Sinaiticus. He also worked out principles of textual criticism and published eight editions of Greek Testaments. The eighth edition, completed in 1872, was a monumental work. Its text is not the best, but it gives a remarkably accurate and full critical apparatus, giving the variant readings of all the important uncials known at the time and many of the cursives. It is still the great standard critical apparatus.

B. F. Westcott, Bishop of Durham, and F. J. A. Hort, Professor of Divinity at Cambridge, produced the best Greek text that has yet been made. After twenty-eight years of work, based on the work of scholars before them, they produced their text in 1881. We have already given a summary of the principles on which they worked. These principles have been studied most critically for over fifty years now, but they have stood the test of time, and scholars today accept all their principles as fundamentally sound. They did not print a critical apparatus with their text. Their text has definitely displaced the old Received Text as the standard text today. Both Westcott and Hort were on the committee to produce the English Revised Version of 1881, and that version and the American Revised Version of 1901 followed the Westcott-Hort text very closely.

H. von Soden brought out a great edition of the Greek New Testament between 1902 and 1911. Great things were expected of this edition, but it was largely a disappointment. Von Soden used different principles, but they have not won the approval of scholars; his text is considered little better than the old Received Text.

He introduced a new system of notation for manuscripts, but it is so complicated that it has not been found useful. His critical apparatus is the best we have for the cursive manuscripts, but inaccuracies and complicated groupings mar it.

In recent years other texts have been produced by various scholars, but, in general, they have accepted the Westcott-Hort principles and have printed substantially the Westcott-Hort text. Notable among these is the Nestle text, now in its sixteenth edition (1936), which gives almost the same text as Westcott and Hort, and in addition gives a splendid brief critical apparatus, giving all the more important variant readings and their attestation in the more important manuscripts. Work is also under way to produce a new full critical apparatus to bring the eighth edition of Tischendorf up to date. As yet only the Gospel of Mark has appeared, under the editorship of Legg. No attempt has been made to improve upon the Westcott-Hort text; it is printed as such at the top of the page. The critical apparatus is like that of the old Tischendorf, but it includes all the newer uncials and some few of the cursives.

Textual criticism is not a completed task. Splendid work has been done in the past, and we have good reasons for believing that the text which we now have is a highly accurate one. But new manuscripts are still coming to light, and they and others are being more and more completely worked. The Westcott-Hort principles are still being studied critically. Variant theories are still being put forward, most of them, however, dealing with secondary matters. There is debate now as to whether their Neutral text is really an un-edited, neutral text or a text edited on fine textual principles; in either case it is still considered the purest available text. It may be necessary to divide their old Western family further. Theta and the Chester Beatty Papyri have thrown interesting new light on the Caesarean family; however, it is not clear yet as to whether we should consider it a separate family, like the Neutral and Western; or a sub-family having some of the characteristics of both the Neutral and the Western. It looks, though, as if the Westcott-Hort principles will continue to stand in all essential matters; probably little improvement can be expected on the text that they have given us. But the work still goes on. Canon B. H. Streeter of England was laboring in the field of the Caesarean text until his recent death in an aeroplane crash. Professor Kirsopp Lake of Harvard is leading a group that is still working in that field. Professors E. C. Colwell and D. W. Riddle of the University of Chicago have a group of scholars working with them in research in the field of the lectionaries. These medieval lesson-books are expected to throw some interesting light on the development of the medieval text, though they will probably not contribute much towards a better critical text. Textual work is very slow and is highly specialized, and the workers are all too few; but splendid work has been done since the days of the crude Erasmus edition of 1516. Solid foundations have been laid, and a technique has been developed to enable us to handle anything else the future may disclose to us.

III

THE CANON OF THE NEW TESTAMENT

THE word "canon" comes from the Greek word *kanon,* a reed, a rod, a rule, a standard. It has many applications, but we shall use it here as it applies to the authoritative list of books that make up our Bible. There is uniform agreement that there are twenty-seven books in the New Testament. How did just those twenty seven come to constitute our New Testament? Why were there not more or fewer? Why should some books be included and others excluded? We shall be able to give only the outlines of this large subject.

The ultimate test of canonicity is inspiration. If the book in question is "God-breathed" it belongs in the canon; if it is not, it does not. But inspiration is a very intangible thing, so more definite tests were needed. One of the most important tests used was that of apostolicity; was the book the work of an apostle? Some books included in the canon were not actually written by apostles, as Mark and Luke-Acts; but they had apostolic authority back of them, such as Peter's and Paul's. The test of usefulness played its part. Not all of the writings of all of the apostles went into the New Testament, but only those that were useful enough to the Church to warrant their preservation. Then there were the tests of doctrine and morality; some books were excluded because the doctrine and morality taught were not in harmony with the thought of the true Church. So we see that the ultimate test was intangible and that several secondary tests were used. Naturally, for a time there was disagreement in the application of these tests. After several centuries, however, there came agreement, and for fifteen hundred years there has been no serious attempt to change the canon of the New Testament.

The Bible of the early Christian Church was the Old Testament. The writers of the New Testament books wrote their books one at a time to meet certain specific needs. They probably had no idea that their books would finally come together and make a collection on a par with the Old Testament. The books were written by many different men at different times to different churches all over the Roman Empire. When the books began to circulate, they circulated quite independently. But after a while the books began, in the providence of God, to come together, probably in smaller groups. Our four gospels came together and were put in a class separate from all other gospel writings. Probably a collection of the letters of Paul followed the publication of the life of Paul in Acts. Then there was made a collection of the General Epistles. Finally these groups were put together and Acts and Revelation added to complete our New Testament.

To trace the development of the canon, we must go first to the writings of the early Christian Fathers. In the earliest period there are no lists of canonical books; we must study the writings of the Fathers and see what books they used as their authorities. At times this is a bit uncertain. We cannot be sure that a Father considered a book uncanonical just because we can find no use of it in his extant writings. At times we cannot be sure whether a Father is using a book as authoritative or simply using it as he would any other book.

But at a later period the Fathers begin to discuss definitely the problems of the canon and make lists of books that they consider canonical. Finally the councils of the Church take up the matter and issue their pronouncements. We note that the councils come at the end, not the beginning.

EXTRA-CANONICAL BOOKS

We are all familiar with the twenty-seven books that now make up our New Testament. It may be well to look briefly at some of the other books that were considered worthy of consideration as the canon was being formed.

The *Didache*, or *Teaching of the Twelve Apostles*, is a collection of sayings of Jesus and directions for church worship and practice. It claims to have been written by the twelve apostles, but the claim is manifestly false. It is to be dated probably between 100 and 150 A. D., though it may have come from an even earlier Jewish work. Most of the material that is of any value comes from our four gospels, especially Matthew. Some parts of it are very good and interesting; others, rather puerile. The book was widely circulated, but only in Egypt does it ever seem to have been considered canonical; Clement of Alexandria and Origen seem to have considered it so.

The *Epistle of Barnabas* was probably written between 100 and 130. It is an interesting document but of no real importance. It, too, was probably considered canonical by some of the Egyptians. Clement commented on it in his *Hypotyposes*, or commentary on the Catholic Epistles. Origen called it "Catholic." It is found in the great New Testament manuscript Aleph, which probably came from Egypt.

The *First Epistle of Clement* was written by Clement of Rome, from Rome to Corinth, about 96. It is an early, interesting document of the early Church. It was included in the manuscript Alexandrinus, or "A," and a few secondary manuscripts. Irenaeus, Clement of Alexandria, and Origen all use it, but they do not seem to put it on a par with the canonical writings.

The *Shepherd of Hermas* seems to have been written in Rome about 150. It is a rather long work, purporting to give much teaching and revelation about the future. Irenaeus, Tertullian, and Clement of Alexandria all use it, probably as Scripture. But shortly after their time, it was attacked as immoral and its authority denied. Thereafter it was not considered canonical, but it was frequently spoken of as a useful book for Christian study.

The *Apocalypse of Peter* was probably written in the early second century and only falsely assigned to the Apostle. It claims to give a revelation of the future. It describes heaven and hell, especially the latter. It goes into all the gruesome details of the punishments that are supposed to be meted out to the different classes of sinners. It was widely used, especially in Egypt. Clement of Alexandria commented on it in his *Hypotyposes*. It is placed in a secondary position in several of the canonical lists.

The *Acts of Paul* was written about 160 by a Presbyter of Asia, in honor of Paul. According to Tertullian, he was convicted of imposture and degraded from his office. There are quite a few interesting stories in what we have left of the book, but at best their historical value is exceedingly doubtful. Origen and Clement of Alexandria cited it with respect. The Syrian Church of the fourth century thought highly of it; Ephraem commented on it. It was known in the West but not considered canonical.

There were many other later books of all kinds, gospels, acts, epistles, and apocalypses, assigned to many of the apostles; but the Church did not give serious consideration to them.

The Syrian Church

The Syrian Church started with a small canon and gradually worked up to our present canon.

The early Syriac canon included the *Diatessaron*, the Pauline Epistles, and Acts. The *Diatessaron* (from the Greek "through four") was a kind of harmony or interweaving of our four gospels into one, made by Tatian.

The canon of the Peshitto Syriac, a translation probably made by Rabbula, Bishop of Edessa, in the early fifth century, included twenty-two books: the four gospels, Acts, fourteen letters of Paul, James, I Peter, and I John. The minor Catholic Epistles and Revelation were omitted. The great Chrysostom of Constantinople followed this same canon.

The Philoxenian Syriac, a translation made about 508, has our complete list of twenty-seven books.

The Egyptian Church

The Egyptian Church started with a large canon and gradually worked down to our present canon.

Most of the books that were considered canonical anywhere were considered canonical in Egypt, as we have seen above.

Clement of Alexandria comments on several of the extra-canonical books in his *Hypotyposes* and seems to use others as canonical in his writings, including I Clement, Barnabas, the Apocalypse of Peter, and the Shepherd of Hermas.

Origen was the head of the catechetical school at Alexandria and wrote freely during the first half of the third century. He divided the canon into two classes of books, the acknowledged and the disputed. The acknowledged list included: four gospels, thirteen Pauline epistles, I Peter, I John, Acts, and Revelation. The disputed list included: Hebrews, II Peter, II and III John, James, Jude, Barnabas, Hermas, Didache, and the gospel of the Hebrews. It is a question how many of these disputed books Origen himself considered canonical, probably most or all of them.

Eusebius, who wrote his *Church History* about 325, divided the canon into three classes, those acknowledged by all, those disputed but known to most (and probably accepted by him), and those disputed but rejected. The acknowledged group was: the four gospels, Acts, fourteen Paulines, I John, I Peter, Revelation ("if it seems proper"). The disputed but accepted list contained James, Jude, II Peter, II and III John. The disputed but rejected list included: Acts of Paul, Hermas, the Apocalypse of Peter, Barnabas, Didache, Revelation ("if it seems proper"), and the gospel of the Hebrews. It is strange that he puts Revelation in the first and third lists instead of the second. If we put his first two lists together, we get our canon of twenty-seven books.

The great manuscript Sinaiticus, or Aleph, which was probably written in Egypt about 350, contains our twenty-seven books plus Barnabas and Hermas.

In the year 367, Athanasius' Easter letter to the Egyptian Christians said that our twenty-seven books, and they alone, were to be considered canonical. This is the earliest definite list of just our canon. Catechumens were permitted to read the Didache and Hermas.

The Roman Church

The Roman Church followed a middle course and stayed rather close to our present canon until it was definitely reached.

About 140, the Gnostic heretic, Marcion, put forth a very small canon of books consistent with his doctrine and his hostility to the Old Testament, including only Luke and the ten Pauline epistles. He rejected from the Paulines the Pastoral Epistles and Hebrews and called Ephesians Laodiceans. The fact that the heretic, Marcion, had tried to substitute a manifestly defective canon made the orthodox see the necessity of forming a true canon and system of doctrine.

Towards the end of the second century, Irenaeus, bishop of Lyons, quotes freely from most of our New Testament books, definitely from the four gospels, Acts, the Paulines, I Peter, I and II John, and Revelation.

Tertullian, Presbyter of Carthage in the early third century, quotes freely from the gospels, Acts, all the Paulines except Philemon, Hebrews (as Barnabas'), I Peter, I John, Jude, and Revelation.

The Muratorian Canonical Fragment, which probably comes from Rome about 200, gives the following list: the gospels, Acts, thirteen Paulines (Laodiceans and Alexandrians — probably Hebrews — are spurious), Jude, I and II John, Wisdom of Solomon, Revelation of John, Revelation of Peter (which some reject); Hermas may be read privately.

Cyprian of Carthage, about the middle of the third century, lacked Philemon, Hebrews, James, II Peter, II and III John, and Jude. All of these are very short except Hebrews, and their omission may have been accidental. Hebrews was slow winning its way at Rome because of its doubtful authorship.

After Cyprian, all the West had at least all the

books he had. Gradually the minor books won their places. The authority of Augustine and Jerome finally assured Hebrews of its place; they were convinced of its Pauline authority if not of its actual Pauline authorship.

The Councils

The earlier councils had nothing of any value to say on the subject of the canon. When the councils did begin to take action, the usage of the Church, as we have traced it, had already decided the matter. The councils merely put their stamp of approval on what had already been done and assured an authoritative uniformity.

The Council of Laodicea, in 363, was the first council to take definite action on the canon. Its Canon 59 ordered that only canonical books be read in church. The canonical books were not listed, it being probably assumed that they were well known. The so-called Canon 60, with its list of twenty-six books, omitting Revelation, has been rather definitely proved spurious.

The Council of Hippo, in 393, took action on the matter, but its canons are fragmentary. However, its Canon 36 is known to have been the same as that of the Council of Carthage, in 397.

The Council of Carthage, in 397, gives a canonical list of exactly our twenty-seven books. It is interesting to notice, however, that we have this strange note: "Epistles of Paul, thirteen; Epistle of same to the Hebrews, one."

The Council of Carthage, in 419, gives our twenty-seven books, including simply "Epistles of Paul, fourteen."

These were local synods, but the Fourth Ecumenical Council at Chalcedon, in 451, and the Council of Trullo, in 692, ratified their work.

The Council of Trent, the Thirty-nine Articles, the Gallican Articles, the Belgic Confession, and the Westminster Confession list the twenty-seven books by name. The Lutheran Confessions refer to them without naming them.

The development of the canon may seem haphazard and indefinite, but we believe that the providence of God was back of it, guiding the Church to the selection of just those books that His Spirit had inspired. Are we in doubt about what we now have? Is there a single book that we would be willing to lose from our New Testament? On the other hand, read the extra-canonical books and see if there is one that you would be willing to put on a par with the books of our New Testament. No, God does not always lead the Church infallibly; but we do believe that He did eventually lead it unerringly to just those books that He wanted in His New Covenant. And the history of fifteen hundred years points to the same conclusion.

IV

THE LANGUAGE OF THE NEW TESTAMENT

Greek or Aramaic ?

For centuries it had been universally believed that all the books of the New Testament were written originally in Greek. In recent years certain attempts have been made to prove that some of the books were written in Aramaic, then later translated into Greek. Aramaic was a language of the Semitic family, related to the Hebrew of the Old Testament, which was in common use among the Jews of Palestine of the first century. Almost certainly Jesus and the apostles ordinarily spoke Aramaic; but almost certainly they knew Greek, which was the universal language of the time.

The attempt to prove an Aramaic original has centered around the Fourth Gospel, though some have included all four of the gospels and the first half of Acts.[1]

In trying to prove the Aramaic origins, certain

[1] For the Aramaic origins, cf. C. F. Burney, **The Aramaic Origin of the Fourth Gospel,** 1922; J. A. Montgomery, **The Origin of the Gospel According to St. John,** 1923; and C. C. Torrey, **The Aramaic Origin of the Fourth Gospel** in **Harvard Theological Review,** 1923, and **The Four Gospels, a New Translation,** 1933. For the best refutation cf. E. C. Colwell, **The Greek of the Fourth Gospel,** 1931; this applies primarily to the Fourth Gospel, but the conclusions apply even more strongly to the others. See also, E. J. Goodspeed, **New Chaps. in N. T. Study,** 1937, chap. VI, for a brief refutation of Aramaic origin theories for practically all books of the N. T.

scholars have picked out certain phenomena in the book or books in question and have asserted that they are not good Greek but show signs of translation. Take some of these strange phenomena and translate them literally into Aramaic, and the Aramaic is perfectly smooth and idiomatic. Sometimes, it is asserted, the Greek makes no sense; but if we translate it as it stands into Aramaic, we can see that the Aramaic, as it stands or very slightly changed, can mean something else that does make sense. Burney, Torrey, and Montgomery make much of these alleged rough translations and mistranslations.

Colwell has made a careful study of their claims. He has put the alleged mistranslations of the three scholars in parallel columns, and he has found that they do not agree among themselves, but, rather, contradict each other freely. He has taken the phenomena that were claimed to be rough Greek but good Aramaic grammar and has paralleled practically every one from the Greek of the papyri and Epictetus, the common Greek of the period, which certainly had no Aramaic original; many of them were found even in good Classical Greek.

While the problem is primarily a technical, grammatical one, it may be said that the historical probabilities are strongly against the Aramaic origin theories also. By the time the gospels were written, there were large numbers of Gentiles in the Church, and the Church was seeking to win even more. The gospels were written as missionary literature, and it is certain that the Greek language was far more useful for the purpose than the Aramaic. Not a single copy of an Aramaic gospel has survived, if there ever was one; those who favor the Aramaic origin theory must get their Aramaic "original" by translating the Greek back into Aramaic, and, of course, no two do it alike.

The theory of an Aramaic original for any of the New Testament books has not been proved; in fact, it has been rather positively disproved. Were such a theory proved, it would be necessary to make a rather thorough reconstruction of much of New Testament introduction, including, especially, questions of date, authorship, and origins, and the whole synoptic problem. We, of course, expect certain Aramaic touches in literature written by Jews. Greek was a secondary language for the Jews of the first century, and naturally the Greek that they wrote would have a certain Aramaic flavor. Admitting that, however, is far from admitting that the books were written in Aramaic and then translated into Greek.

The question of the original language of the sayings of Jesus is one that cannot be fully determined. The probability is that He knew both Greek and Aramaic and that He used both. Normally, in speaking to a Jewish group, He would use the Aramaic. Probably some of the early collections of the sayings, back of the gospels, were written in Aramaic. Any light that the Aramaic can throw on the original force and meaning of the sayings will be welcome.

Characteristics of New Testament Greek

The New Testament was not written in Classical Greek. For a long time it was thought that the New Testament Greek was simply a crude mixture of Greek and Aramaic, Semitic idioms written in Greek letters. The German scholar, Deissmann[2] was largely responsible for changing this old view. He made a study of the Greek papyri that were being found in such large numbers in Egypt, where they had been preserved through the ages by the dry sand. He found that the

[2] **Bibelstudien**, 1895; **Licht vom Osten**, 1908; translated into English as **Bible Studies** and **Light from the Ancient East**.

Greek of the papyri that could be dated around the time of the New Testament was just the same as the Greek of the New Testament itself. Deissmann's conclusions have been thoroughly proved by the further grammatical study of the twentieth century. Now all grammarians believe that the New Testament was written in the common Greek dialect that was in use all over the Roman Empire at the time of Christ, which we call the "Koine," from the Greek word meaning "common."

When Philip of Macedon and Alexander the Great went forth on their conquests in the fourth century B.C., they undertook to spread the Greek culture and language wherever they went. They and their successors carried out their policies so well that the Greek language came to be used, at least as a secondary language, throughout the whole Mediterranean world. The fact of this universal language was a marvelous preparation for the spread of Christianity; missionaries did not have to go to language school when they entered a new country; Paul, with a knowledge of just Greek, could go anywhere he wanted and get a hearing. The books of the New Testament written in Greek could be read by the whole Church.

Philip and Alexander started to spread the Attic dialect of the Classical Greek, the one with which they were most familiar. It was too complicated a language to be used as it stood by the common people, as a secondary language. Naturally, some of its fine points passed out of use. Then, of course, no language is a static thing; English, today, is quite different from what it was in Shakespeare's time. The Koine Greek is a lineal descendant from the Classical Attic Greek, though certain rather striking changes have taken place. And, of course, we expect to find some influence on the Greek coming from the primary language of the person who is using it.

When we compare the Koine with the Classical Greek, we see that there has been, in general, a simplification of sentence structure and forms. The Koine does not have so many long complex sentences. It no longer uses the dual number in nouns and verbs. The old optative mood has almost gone; it is used just a few times, mostly in wishing clauses. The old *-mi* verbs are giving way before the newer, more regular *-o* verbs. The use of *hina* clauses is being greatly extended beyond the Classical purpose clause. The negative *me* has displaced the *ou* from use with almost everything except the indicative mood. Particles are used with less frequency and accuracy.

Since the New Testament Greek has been put in its proper place, much scientific grammatical and lexicographical work has been done. Comparative historical grammar shed much valuable light from time to time. New papyri are still coming to light, and those that we have are being studied more thoroughly. Interesting and helpful new light is being shed on certain words whose meanings have been vague or uncertain. New Testament Greek is a fascinating, live study today.[3]

[3] For a fuller treatment of the history and characteristics of the Koine Greek, cf. A. T. Robertson, **A Grammar of the Greek New Testament in the Light of Historical Research,** part I.

V

PAGAN RELIGIONS IN THE ROMAN EMPIRE

CHRISTIANITY did not come into a world devoid of religions. The people of the first century had many, many religions. Christianity had strenuous competition from the very first. One by one these pagan religions gave way to the superior religion, until finally Christianity became the official religion of the Roman Empire in the fourth century under Constantine. The student of the New Testament and of the history of the early Christian Church needs something of an understanding of these many religions that played such an important part in the lives of the first century peoples to whom Christianity was given as the better, the final religion.

THE GREEK RELIGION

Greek religion was a poetical polytheism. It worshiped nature with its visible objects and invisible powers in an anthropomorphic way. The gods and goddesses were living realities to the Greeks; they had human strength and wisdom and virtues to a high degree; they also excelled in human vices.

All of us are more or less familiar with the myths of Greece. Homer, with his *Iliad* and *Odyssey*, may almost be considered the Greek Bible. The Greek dramatists, Aeschylus, Sophocles, Euripides, and the others, got their themes largely from their religion. We have the stories of Zeus, the father of the gods; his wife, Hera; his brother, Poseidon, the shaker of the earth, the ruler of the sea and all the waters of the earth; Apollo, the sun, the god of the chase, of poetry and song; of Hephaestus, the blacksmith; of Ares, the god of war; Hermes, the messenger; Athene, the goddess of wisdom; Artemis, the goddess of the chase; Aphrodite, the goddess of beauty and love; and countless others.

The divinities of old Greece were divided into two classes, the Olympian and the Chthonian, the heavenly and the earthly, the gods and the demons. From the Olympian deities comes all that is good—wisdom, happiness, prosperity, unity, beauty, song. From the hard gods comes all that is evil—sickness of body and mind, crime, remorse, punishment, lamentation, mourning, and woe. Zeus was honored when all went well, but in times of trouble, the Greek turned not to the god but to the devil.

Sacrifice, augury, and magic played a large part in the religious life of the Greeks. Morality played no part at all. If the Greeks had imitated many of the practices of their gods, they would have been much more immoral than they were. There was no hope of personal communion with the gods. The mystical element was largely lacking. Practically no light was thrown on the mystery of the life after death. The problem of sin may have been felt by some of the Greeks, but the Greek religion had no solution to offer for it.

With the rise of Greek philosophy, about the fourth century B.C., the Greek religion began to decline. The philosophers were impressed with the unity of the universe; monotheism became the only tenable philosophical system. Some of the philosophers simply discarded the old religion and tried to laugh it out of court. Others seemed to hold on to it after a fashion, building their monotheism around Zeus. The nobler minds among the Greeks had been repulsed by the immorality of the gods, also. Some of the dramatists, notably Euripides, joined the philosophers in their fight against the old religion. Yet the ideas of the philosophers never came to be the ideas of the masses. The old religion declined; it came to be less and less universally accepted; but we may be sure that it was still an important factor in the first century of the Christian era. In Paul's day Athens was still full of temples and altars; Paul said that the Athenians were a very religious people.

In the Greek religion it was customary that the various cities should have certain ones of the gods and goddesses as patrons, to whom special honor and reverence was to be given. Athene was the patron goddess of Athens; Artemis, of Ephesus; Poseidon and Aphrodite, of Corinth; and so on.

The Roman Religion

The old Roman faith was remarkably simple. There was hardly any mythology, and for a long time the gods had no statues. It was also strongly moral; the gods gave every man his duty and expected him to perform it. Obedience to parents, purity, decency, respect for law, diligence, patriotism — all these were good old Roman virtues, commanded by the gods and enforced by the censors. It was a respectable, prosaic religion of men who were too busy to have any time for sentiment.

When Rome became the mistress of the world, there was, no doubt, a change. The gods of Greece found their way into Roman life along with Greek culture and Greek vices. The old Roman gods were identified with the Greek gods who possessed, roughly, analogous functions. Jupiter was identified with Zeus; Juno, with Hera; Neptune, with Poseidon; Vulcan, with Hephaestus; Mars, with Ares; Mercury, with Hermes; Minerva, with Athene; Diana, with Artemis; Venus, with Aphrodite; and so on down the line. The cold and lifeless Roman gods and goddesses began to take on the beauty and grace of their Greek counterparts. Yet the Greek ideas never quite took the place of the old Roman ones. Educated Romans never treated the Greek religion very seriously. Soldiers looked for victory to the gods of the standards. The common people still turned to the Pales and the homely deities of the fields.

As in the case of the Greek religion, with the rise of philosophy, the Roman religion also began to decline. But as unbelief grew, there grew also, in like proportion, pomp and stateliness and luxury of public worship. There came to be many augurs, oracle-keepers, banquet-masters, and all kinds of priests. Temples, altars, festivals, and ceremonies multiplied. The clergy became less moral and more political and worldly.

In the first century of the Christian era, Roman religion developed a new feature, Caesar worship. Starting first with the deification of dead rulers, by gradual steps, the living emperors came to be worshiped throughout the empire as "saviors." For a time the emperors paid little attention to this feature, but by the end of the century the demand that all worship the image of the Emperor Domitian produced the crisis in the Christian Church which gave rise to the Book of Revelation.

The Mystery Religions

We have noticed the decline of both the Greek and the Roman religions. Philosophers wanted monotheism.

The whole world was becoming unified and travel was easy, so travelers became dissatisfied with local divinities and wanted a universal god. Then there began to grow up a great desire for purity, repentance, atonement, and expiation. The Greeks had attributed these to the demons, and the Latins had largely ignored them. Men began to require a new god who could give meaning to their lives and guide them to some profitable end. What we know as the mystery religions came in to make a bid to fulfill these needs of mankind.

There were many mystery religions, but they all had certain things in common. They made much of drama and symbolism. They all claimed to provide salvation for man, to remove the estrangement between man and God, to enable man to live the full life on earth and secure for him a blessed immortality. They were all personal religions; a man became a member by his own choice, not by accident of birth. They all claimed to be universal, not local or national, religions. They were not narrow, exclusive religions; one person could be in good standing in many mysteries at the same time.

Most of the mysteries seem to have had three stages in their ritual.

First, there was a period of preparation and probation. The seeker must take vows of secrecy; he must make confession of his sins, undergo baptisms or purifications according to carefully prescribed forms, offer sacrifices of various kinds, and undergo ascetic preparations of all kinds and degrees of rigor—prolonged fasts, absolute continence, severe bodily mutilations, uncomfortable pilgrimages to holy places, public confession, and so on.

Second, comes the period of initiation and communion. After due probation, the neophyte was solemnly received into membership of the cult and into fellowship with its members and its deity. Naturally, we know less about the process of initiation proper than about other parts of the mysteries; the rites could not be divulged. The nearest approach to an unveiling of the secret is found in Apuleius' strange words concerning the Isis cult[1]: "Hear, therefore, but believe what is true. I approached the confines of Death and trod the threshold of Proserpina; I was carried through all the elements and returned again; in the middle of the night I saw the sun gleaming in radiant splendor, I approached into the presence of the gods below and the gods celestial and worshiped before their face. Behold, I have told you things which, although you have heard them, you must not understand." It is possible that in this second stage, in some of the mysteries at least, there occurred such rites as the taurobolium, regeneration, communion and identification with the god, a mystery-marriage, and so on.

The third stage, or the result of the other two, was the *epopteia* of the Mystery-god; the deity granted an appearance to the faithful. Blessedness and salvation in general were supposed to follow this, for this life and the life to come.

Besides these things held in common, each mystery had its own set of gods and goddesses and its own myths and ritual.

The Greek Mysteries

At an early date the mystery element made its appearance in connection with the Greek god Dionysius, god of wine, the Latin Bacchus. The worshipers in this cult sought to attain contact with the god partly by a divine frenzy, which was induced by wild music and dancing, and partly by the crass method of eating the raw flesh of the sacred animal, the bull.

---

[1] Met. XI, 23.

Related in some way to the Dionysian cult was the Orphic cult, based on the Greek Orpheus, the mystical musician and seer. Possibly this was an attempt to reform away some of the worst elements of the worship of Dionysius. Orphism is especially important because it taught men to expect in the future life not only rewards but also punishments. The soul after death was subject to an indefinite succession of reincarnations, not only in the bodies of men, but also in those of animals. At last the righteous soul attains purification and enters into a blessed existence.

Another cult among the Greek mysteries was that of Eleusis, a town of Attica about fifteen miles from Athens. This was based on the worship of Demeter and her daughter Persephone. It was carried on with remarkable elaborateness in the city of Athens and gave rise to some of the greatest Greek dramas and festivals, but it does not seem to have spread at all widely.

The Eastern Mysteries

I. *Isis.* The worship of Isis originated in Egypt, but it spread in the early Christian era all over the Roman Empire, even to Britain. The myth on which the ritual was based had to do with Isis and her husband Osiris, or Serapis. Osiris, while still king upon earth, had been hailed as a deity because of the beneficence of his rule and his skill in encouraging the growth of wheat, barley, and the vine. Arousing the envy of his brothers, Set and Typhon, he was put to death by them; and his body, enclosed in a coffin, floated out to sea. Typhon, coming upon the body unexpectedly, rent it into fourteen pieces. Isis, in grief, wandered everywhere seeking the body of her lover. At last, as she was sailing up and down the Nile in a boat made of papyrus, she found the fourteen pieces. Weeping, she placed them in order, and, breathing and mourning over them, finally restored them to life. Osiris revived and reigned as king of the dead, bearing the titles of Lord of the Underworld, Lord of Eternity, and Ruler of the Dead.

The Isis cult made a very strong appeal because of its promise of resurrection and immortality. Then there was its impressive antiquity, coming out of mystical Egypt. Then the priesthood, unlike those of Greek and Roman temples, was a class apart, wholly devoted to the service of the gods. The worship was not a matter of holidays, but a perpetual round of rites and litanies; every morning the shrine was opened with offerings and prayers; every evening it was closed with like solemn ceremonies. On stated days, though, there were great processions through the streets, which served to attract new members.

There were some rather noble and attractive features in the worship of Isis, but there were also many extremely repulsive, unmentionable features. The central idea of death and resurrection was associated with the reproduction in nature and mankind, and this emphasis gave rise to much that we must abhor.

II. *Mithra.* The worship of Mithra came from Persia. We cannot be sure how important it had become in the first Christian century, but it soon became Christianity's most important rival, the religion that Christianity finally overcame only in the fourth century.

Mithra was a Persian deity, but in the original Persian religion of Mazda he plays only a subordinate part. In the Mithra cult he becomes the central figure. He is always pictured as a young man wearing Persian clothes.

The missionaries of the cult seem to have been mainly soldiers, who were well fitted for this task because of their wide travels. Wherever the Roman legions were quartered or trade was active, there the temples of the Persian deity occur in great numbers.

In primitive times Mithra appears to have been worshiped in grottoes among the rocks, and, wherever his religion spread, the ancient usage was kept in mind by the peculiar construction of his temples, which were subterranean, and were always called caves. Along the side walls of one of these caves ran a sloping bench of stone, on which the worshipers knelt. In this same hut, there were three altars and various sculptures. It was a very small place and could not have accommodated more than forty or fifty worshipers at a time. Running water was necessary for the ritual.

In the old Iranian theology, Mithra was by no means the sovereign figure. The highest place belongs to Zervan or Eternity, beneath whom stand Ormuzd, the great father of all that exists, and his opposite, Ahriman, the spirit of evil. Between these two there is incessant war. Here we meet again the metaphysical, pantheistic thought of Eternity, the hostility between the champions of good and evil, and the legible traces of a primitive nature worship. Although Mithra was originally but one among the lower gods of Persia, his figure is of such force and vitality and has been animated by such profoundly religious conceptions, that he pushes all the others into the background and remains the one sufficient object of worship. He is the mediator between god and man, creator, regenerator, the giver of all light, the champion of justice, truth, and holiness, the comforter of man in all trouble, and his strong helper against the evil Ahriman, who by his grace can always be overcome.

Many myths grew up around Mithra. Especially popular were the stories of his birth, his slaying the bull, his feasting with the Sun, and his various labors in behalf of man.

The ritual and priesthood were highly developed. All of the widespread churches seem to have been bound together by some kind of federation. Only men were admitted to membership.

III. *Cybele*. Corresponding to the Mithra cult for the men was the cult of the Phrygian goddess, the Great Mother Cybele. This was one of the first of the Eastern mysteries to invade the west, and, along with Mithraism, was the last to give way to Christianity. The inhabitants of Phrygia had always been renowned for their excitability, and their religion, based upon emotionalism, and characterized by violent ecstasies, was often accompanied by orgies of a peculiarly revolting kind.

Nature worship was the foundation of this cult. Attis, a young herdsman, beloved by Cybele, the mother of all fertility, in repentance for faithlessness, unmanned himself under a pine tree and there died of his wound. Cybele, in wild grief, rushed through woods and mountains, bewailing with piercing cries the loss of her lover. But Attis rose to life again and was restored to the bosom of his mourning lover, who was also, as some believed, his mother. Thus was symbolized the death of vegetation in autumn, the raging of the winter storm, and the return of fertility to the earth with spring and summer.

The Emperor Claudius (41-54 A.D.) introduced the Spring Festival in honor of Attis and Cybele, which lasted from the 22nd to the 27th of March. With wonderful and striking pageantry the priests of Cybele celebrated the death, burial, and resurrection of Attis and the joy of his lover at his return. This festival, and indeed the whole worship of Cybele, was bound up with shameful orgiastic rites. But beneath all these shameful rites, the devotees sought ever more earnestly for a new spiritual message, for purification from sin and a life beyond the grave.

IV. *Adonis.* Very little is known about the Phoenician Adonis cult. The myth is that the youth Adonis, beloved by Aphrodite, was killed by a wild boar, and then bemoaned by the goddess. At Byblos in Phoenicia, the death and resurrection of the god are yearly celebrated with secret ritual, accompanied by wailing and mourning. When those who participated in it have finished their mourning, they sacrifice in the place to Adonis, as to one who has departed this life. Then they allege that he is alive again and exhibit his effigy to the sky. Something of this nature may have been done elsewhere in the Roman Empire.

Christianity and the Pagan Religions

These religions made very little impression on the natives of Palestine. Attempts were made from time to time to force some of these religions on the Jews, but the Jews stoutly resisted; they had a holy hatred of all gods other than Jehovah. But the Jews in the Dispersion, in the midst of the Gentile world, probably had quite a bit of contact with these pagan religions.

Christianity started as a Jewish movement, but it soon turned to the Gentiles, until it finally became a Gentile movement. Probably most of the Gentiles who became Christians in the first century came from these pagan religions. At times they brought into their Christianity some relics of their paganism. For example, we know that grave problems were raised in the Church of Corinth because of the emotionalism and sexual emphasis that the members had received from their pagan background.

As the Christian missionaries sought to extend their message among the Gentiles, we may be sure that they made use of concepts that were familiar to the Gentiles. It is a question how far the early Christians borrowed elements of importance from the mysteries especially.

Some scholars have gone to such extremes as to say that all of the essential points of Paul's concept of Christianity were taken from the mysteries; Paul makes of Christianity just a Christ-cult, just another one of the mysteries. Such extreme claims cannot be proved; to do so, it must be proved that the features in question were in existence during the time of Paul, at a place where Paul could have used them, and that he actually did use them; we must prove that Paul borrowed from the mysteries rather than that the mysteries borrowed from Paul. From time to time, Paul does seem to use some of the familiar terminology of the mysteries, stating the truths of Christianity in language that his hearers understood. The mysteries especially had their part to play in preparing the way for the spread of the Christian gospel. They had made the world familiar with religions that claimed to be universal instead of the old national religions. They had made the Gentile world familiar with the union of religion and morality, conscious of the problem of sin, desirous of obtaining salvation in this life and the life to come. They made men want the things that Christianity could give. They claimed to give them too, but the test of time proved that only Christianity's claims were true; they passed away—Christianity lives on.

PART TWO
SPECIAL INTRODUCTION

VI

THE SYNOPTIC GOSPELS

The Synoptic Problem

The gospels according to Matthew, Mark, and Luke are called the "synoptic gospels" because they "look together" at the life of Jesus. They have many features in common among themselves that they do not share with the Fourth Gospel. How is it that these synoptics have so many points in common? How, also, can their differences be explained?

All of these three gospels give the same general outline of the life of Christ. Frequently all three will give just the same order of events for long sections. Where one of the three takes a different order for a little while, the other two will almost invariably be together; and almost invariably one of the others will be found in agreement with Mark.

We also find the synoptic gospels agreeing among themselves in the selection of the different incidents in the life of Jesus. Almost all of the events told in the shorter Mark are found in either Matthew or Luke, most of them in both. Anyone who will look at all carefully at a harmony of the gospels in either Greek or English can see these similarities in the synoptics and can see that the Fourth Gospel is an entirely different picture.

Probably the most significant similarities, however, are those that can be seen only in Greek. When these similar stories are told in the different gospels, often the very same words are used. Students of Greek who have access to a Greek harmony of the synoptics can see these facts for themselves if they will adopt some such mechanical plan as the following: Underline in Matthew *or* Luke words that are the same as the parallel words in Mark. Underline in Matthew *and* Luke words that are common to both that are not found in Mark. Use two different colors for the underlining, say red for the first class and black for the second. Where the words are not identical but are highly similar, a broken line may be used. When you have gone through the synoptics in some such way as this, you discover some very significant facts. Some results of a study of the Westcott and Hort Greek text as it is presented in Burton and Goodspeed's *Harmony of the Synoptic Gospels in Greek* are as follows:

The following is a list of exactly identical verses (in these figures there must be a complete verse in at least one of the gospels):

Matthew	Mark	Luke
3: 3b	1: 3	3: 4b
15: 9	7: 7	
15: 32b	8: 2	
	10: 15	18: 17
	11: 15b	19: 45
22: 44	12: 36b	
10: 22a	13: 13a	21: 17
24: 16	13: 14b	21: 21a
24: 19	13: 17	
26: 30	14: 26	
7: 7		11: 9b
7: 8		11: 10
8: 9		7: 8
12: 30		11: 23
12: 41		11: 32
13: 42		13: 28a
27: 58a		23: 52

While perfect accuracy is not claimed for these figures, they show that three of the verses are found in identical form in all three synoptics, while fourteen more are found in two gospels.

But these identical verses tell but a small part of the story. Far more verses are found that are almost identical, where there is a slight difference in the order of the words, where a synonym will be inserted, or an alternate grammatical form will be used.

When a teacher is correcting examination papers and finds two that have some answers that are verbally identical or nearly so, he is very suspicious that some copying has been done somewhere. Scholars studying the synoptic gospels feel that such facts as have been pointed out need some explanation.

For a time the attempt was made to account for these facts by the remarkably retentive memories of the Orientals, but very few now think that that theory can explain how the three evangelists followed so closely the same order of events, used so many of the same incidents, and had so many verbal identities and similarities, especially when the Fourth Gospel is so different.

Most critics of the New Testament now believe that it is almost certain that some copying was done somewhere, that some of the gospel writers used other gospels, or that they had access to common sources. There is now almost universal agreement as far as the following two-document hypothesis goes.*

---

* Dom John Chapman in his **Matthew, Mark and Luke,** Longmans, 1937, makes a laborious effort to defend this theory: Matthew was the first gospel, written in Aramaic and later translated into Greek. Peter used Matthew in his preaching, and Mark's gospel was made from Peter's preaching. Luke used both Matthew and Mark. Chapman's arguments are far from conclusive. His theory does not seem to account for the facts nearly so well as the generally accepted two- and multiple document theories. It is still far easier to see why Matthew added much of Jesus' teaching to Mark than to see why Mark omitted it from Matthew, and why Matthew improved Mark's rough Greek rather than the reverse.

Mark was the first of the three gospels to have been written. Both Matthew and Luke had Mark before them and used it freely. They both used Mark for their outlines, inserting their own new material in it in various places. There were no copyright laws, so they appropriated most of Mark's material with little or no change. The red underlining suggested above will be a guide to the study of the use by Matthew and Luke of their first documentary source, Mark. Matthew and Luke frequently make minor changes in Mark so as to present smoother Greek. They frequently change his historical presents into aorists or imperfects. They change his loosely connected coördinate clauses to the smoother subordinate ones. They at times leave out or alter things that may be considered unfitting. For example, Matthew seems to be shielding James and John by making their mother ask for the chief seats for them. In the story of the casting out of the demons, Matthew and Luke omit Mark's "He has Beelzebub," and "For they were saying that he was crazy," probably thinking them derogatory to Jesus. Such facts as Luke's "Great Omission," where he has nothing to parallel Mark 6: 47 - 8: 26, gave rise to a belief that this first synoptic source was an earlier edition of Mark rather than our present gospel, but this "Ur-Markus" theory is not widely held today; it raises more difficulties than it settles. Matthew and Luke seem clearly to have had as their first source a form of Mark, almost, if not exactly, the same as that presented by our best critical texts today.

Matthew and Luke had also in common a second source, from which they both drew material not found in Mark. One who has done the underlining suggested will find that the black underlining will give him a basis for the study of this source. This source has not been preserved through the ages, so that its reconstruction today must be theoretical. There are many things about it that we do not know, such as, who wrote it, where it was written, and when it was written, other than that it was written before Matthew and Luke. Scholars usually refer to this source by the symbol "Q," which is simply the first letter of the German word for source, "Quelle." We cannot be absolutely sure that Q is just one source, but a study of the style of its contents indicates rather clearly its unitary nature. It contains, primarily, sayings of Jesus, so that it is sometimes referred to as the "sayings source." As we do not have the original of this second source, we cannot tell so certainly how Matthew and Luke used it, but they probably used it in much the same way that they used Mark. Canon B. H. Streeter in *The Four Gospels*[1] suggests the following reconstruction of Q (brackets signifying considerable doubt): Luke 3: 2-9, (10-14), 16-17, 21-22; 4:1-16a; 6:20-7:10; 7:18-35; 9:(51-56), 57-60, (61-62); 10:2-16, (17-20), 21-24; 11: 9-52; 12: 1a-12, 22-59; 13: 8-35; 14: 11, 26-27, 34-35; 16: 13, 16-18; 17: 1-6, 20-37; 19: 11-27. This list includes 272 unbracketed verses.

Most scholars now believe that there were other sources besides these two. Luke's introduction tells us of many who have taken in hand to draw up narratives, and he almost certainly used some of them. We go, then, to a multiple-document theory, which includes, but goes beyond, the two-document theory.

There is material in Luke that is not found in Mark or Matthew, which probably came from a special Lukan source, which is usually called "L." A large section

---

[1] Macmillan, 1925, p. 291. Similar reconstructions may be found in Moffatt's **Introduction to the Literature of the N. T.,** 3rd ed., Scribner, 1918, p. 197, and in Harnack's **The Sayings of Jesus,** Putnam, 1906, pp. 127 ff. The latter book is given wholly to the study of the source Q.

of this tells us of Jesus' Perean ministry (9: 57 - 18: 14), so this source is sometimes referred to as "P."

Corresponding to this special Lukan source, we may also posit a special Matthean source, "M."

Then there seem to have been special sources for the infancy narratives. Matthew and Luke had different sources for these, as their accounts show very little similarity. These sources are not usually included in L or M; especially in Luke, the style is so different from the rest of the gospel that this would be almost impossible. Luke's infancy story seems to be a translation from the Aramaic, or at least a most skilful imitation of it. We refer to those sources as Infancy^{M} and Infancy^{L}.

Besides these written sources there were probably others, possibly some more written and, more than likely, some oral.

Such is the multiple-document theory in general. There have been various adaptations of the general theory made from time to time; one of the most famous, that of the Canon Streeter, may be mentioned as an example. The sources of Matthew are very much as the above: Mark, Q, M, and Antiochene Tradition. As Luke does not follow Mark quite as closely as Matthew does, Streeter thinks that there was another document preferred by Luke to Mark, so he changes the reconstruction of the Lucan sources a bit. He thinks that Q and L were combined to make "Proto-Luke," a kind of first edition of the gospel. Proto-Luke was then used as the foundation, and the material from Mark and Infancy^{L} was inserted into it. Streeter gives some rather convincing proof for this extra stage, but his theory has not won general acceptance as yet. [2]

We are not able to find any clear use of written

---

[2] For a very careful study of this and the whole synoptic problem, see B. H. Streeter, **The Four Gospels**, pp. 150 ff.

sources back of the Gospel of Mark. Cadoux[3] has tried to show that our Second Gospel is a combination of three earlier gospels, a Palestinian, a Dispersion, and a Gentile gospel; but his reasoning seems quite subjective, and his whole analysis is far from convincing. We cannot be sure that Mark did not make use of some written sources; but the traditional account, that Mark wrote down what he had heard Peter preach, probably best accounts for most, if not all, of the contents of the gospel.

Oral Sources

Before any of the sources took written form, the gospel material circulated orally. In recent years an attempt has been made to reconstruct the development of the oral tradition. This discipline is called *formgeschichte*, or form criticism. Most of the work in this field has been done by the Germans, Martin Dibelius and Rudolph Bultmann, though B. S. Easton and R. H. Lightfoot have made some contributions, especially in making the material more accessible to English readers.[4] It is difficult enough to be dogmatic about the reconstruction of written sources, so naturally any attempt to reconstruct the development of oral material must be highly theoretical. As yet there is very little agreement among the advocates of this school, and there seems very little likelihood that there can be much agreement.

Each student seeks to pick out what he considers definite forms, in which he thinks oral tradition was

---

[3] A. T. Cadoux, **The Sources of the Second Gospel**, Macmillan.

[4] Dibelius, **Die Formgeschichte des Evangeliums**, 2nd ed., 1933, Eng. trans. **From Tradition to Gospel**, 1934, Nicholson and Watson, London. Bultmann, **Die Geschichte der Synoptischen Tradition**, 2nd ed., 1931. Lightfoot, **History and Interpretation in the Gospels**, Harpers, 1934. Easton, **The Gospel Behind the Gospels**, Scribners, 1927.

handed down: e.g., the early Christian preaching, the paradigm or sayings form, the miracle story, the exhortation, the myth. An attempt is made to arrange the various forms in chronological order, and more credence is given to the earlier forms. Then an attempt is made to separate between the core of the form and the later literary, imaginative trimming wrapped around it. These developed forms were put together, more or less crudely, to form Mark's gospel; some of them may have gone directly into the other synoptics, though written sources account for most of them.

The conclusions reached by the *formgeschichte* scholars have usually been most negative. Bultmann, for example, says that we cannot now make out any clear picture of the life of Jesus, nor can we be sure of a single word He ever spoke.[5] Some scholars seem to think that we can trust just a few of the little historical cores of the earlier forms.

Conservative critics admit freely that the gospel material circulated orally for years before it was written into the gospels or the gospel sources. They do not believe that the *formgeschichte* scholars can afford to be dogmatic about their theoretical reconstructions of the growth of the oral tradition, especially as they are differing so widely among themselves; any certain reconstruction seems an impossibility now. Conservatives deny most emphatically the necessity of reaching such negative conclusions as those reached by the most of the *formgeschichte* scholars; they feel that those conclusions are reached, not from the facts in the case, but from Radical presuppositions as to the historical Jesus and the development of the Christian faith.

As yet, *formgeschichte* is too new for final judgment to be passed upon it. It may prove to be a mere passing

---

5 Bultmann and Kundsin, Form Criticism, trans. by Grant, p. 61.

fad. However, it may be possible for more agreement to be reached, so that it may be carried on further. If so, Conservative scholars may try to carry on work in the field and reach more constructive conclusions in harmony with the Conservative thought about Jesus and early Christianity. For the present, all New Testament scholarship is waiting for more light on this whole field. We are sure that the information circulated orally for a time. If we could reconstruct the course of that tradition, we could get interesting and useful information about the interests of the early Church. But it looks as if an accurate reconstruction is impossible now.[6]

Let it be said that our study of the sources of the synoptics has done nothing to take away any inspiration from them. Inspiration assumes that human beings wrote under divine guidance. Our study has sought to understand the human workings alone.

Authorship

The synoptic gospels, like the Fourth Gospel, the Johannine Epistles, the Epistle to the Hebrews, and many Old Testament books, are anonymous. Of course, tradition has assigned authors' names for most of the anonymous books, but it is the duty of the New Testament scholar to try to see how far the various traditions can be trusted.

The Gospel According to Mark

The earliest manuscripts of our Second Gospel had at the beginning of the gospel the title, "According to

[6] E. Basil Redlich, in his **Form Criticism, Its Value and Limitations,** Scribners, 1939, has made a very fair critique of the limitations of **formgeschichte.** E. F. Scott, in his **The Validity of the Gospel Record,** Scribners, 1938, argues most convincingly for the essential truth of the gospel stories; the very fact of the development of forms even earlier than the written sources proves that the essential facts were preserved and became crystallized at a time when they could be tested.

Mark." As time went on, the title gradually expanded: "The Gospel According to Mark," "The Gospel According to St. Mark," "The Holy Gospel According to St. Mark." Even in its earliest form, however, the title was not a part of the original gospel; it was not written by the author himself but was inserted by some scribe. The titles of the New Testament books do not solve our problems of authorship; they give us simply the traditional view held in certain quarters at the time of the writing of our earliest manuscripts, about the fourth century. But we have tradition that is far earlier than that.

The earliest testimony is that of Papias, Bishop of Hierapolis, from about 140 A.D.[7]: "This also the elder said: Mark, having become Peter's interpreter, wrote down accurately, though not in order, all that he remembered of the things either said or done by Christ. For he was neither a hearer nor a follower of the Lord, but a follower, as I have said, of Peter at a later time; and Peter delivered his instructions to meet the needs of the moment, but with no attempt to give the Lord's words in any systematic arrangement. So that Mark was not wrong in thus writing down some things as he recollected them, for the one thing that he was careful of was to omit nothing of what he had heard or to make any false statement."

About 185 A.D., Irenaeus of Lyons wrote[8]: "After the 'exodus' of these (Peter and Paul), Mark, the disciple and interpreter of Peter, wrote down the things that were being preached by Peter and handed them down to us."

These are the earliest testimonies as to the writer of our Second Gospel, but the same tradition is found

---

[7] Papias, in Eusebius, Church History, 3:39.
[8] Irenaeus 3:1:1, in Eusebius, C. H. 5:8.

time and again in the later writers.[9] The evidence for the Markan authorship is early, and it is unanimous. If an attempt had been made to gain authority for the book by claiming a famous author for it, as was frequently done in the early centuries, no one would have chosen a secondary character like Mark; Peter would have been a far more likely choice. There seems to be not the slightest reason for doubting that Mark wrote the second of our gospels, and that he got his information largely, if not entirely, from the Apostle Peter.

John Mark is one of the interesting minor characters of the New Testament. His mother was a Mary, a Christian whose house was used as an assembly place by the early Church, to which Peter went when he was miraculously released from prison. Mark was at Antioch when that Church sent out the great missionaries, Paul and Barnabas, and Mark went along with them as a helper. They went together through the island of Cyprus, but when they came to the mainland at Perga in Pamphylia, Mark left them and went back to his home in Jerusalem, and the first missionary journey was completed without him. We do not know why Mark left (possibly the journey was proving longer than had been planned, or the going was too hard, or he felt that he was needed at home for some reason), but when the missionaries were making their plans for their second journey and Barnabas wanted to give his cousin Mark another chance, Paul disagreed so violently that he took Silas with him and made his second journey and let Barnabas and Mark go their own ways. They go back to Barnabas' old home, Cyprus, and there Barnabas passes out of the New Testament picture. Mark, however, does not disappear; the failure made good. After the third missionary journey, Paul, in

[9] E. g., Tertullian, Clement of Alexandria, Origen.

prison in Rome, writes to Philemon and the Colossians, and among those sending greetings is Mark, Paul's fellow-worker in the gospel.[10] A little later, when Paul writes his second letter to Timothy, he tells Timothy to come to Rome and bring with him Mark, "for he is profitable to me for the ministry."[11] In I Peter 5: 13 we read: "The church that is at Babylon, elected together with you, saluteth you; and so doth Marcus my son." Peter calls Mark his spiritual son. Mark is with Peter in "Babylon," which is probably Rome, as most scholars have believed at least from the time of Jerome, about 400. So much we learn from the New Testament about Mark. We have already seen the early tradition of his connection with Peter as interpreter and of his writing the gospel. A tradition that can be traced back to the fourth century connects Mark with the founding of the Church in Alexandria;[12] we cannot be so sure about this, however. The fifth century *Paschal Chronicle* says that Mark suffered martyrdom in the time of Trajan (98-117). This failure who made good was the first to write one of our four gospels.

The Gospel According to Matthew

The earliest form of the title of our First Gospel was, "According to Matthew," but we must go back of that.

The earliest testimony comes to us again from Papias of Hierapolis, about 140 A. D.[13]: "Matthew composed the 'logia' in the Hebrew dialect, and each one interpreted them as he was able." Irenaeus, about 185, gave much the same testimony[14]: "Matthew produced a

---

10 Col. 4:12; Philem. 24.

11 II Tim. 4:11.

12 Eusebius, C. H., 2:16,24. Also Jerome, **Apostolic Constitutions,** and Epiphanius.

13 In Eusebius, C. H., 3:39.

14 Irenaeus, 3:1:1 (Eusebius, C. H., 5:8).

gospel writing among the Hebrews in their own language while Peter and Paul were in Rome preaching and founding the Church." Origen, about 250, said that Matthew wrote his Gospel to the Hebrews. Other later writers, such as Eusebius, Cyril of Jerusalem, Epiphanius, and Jerome, give the tradition that Matthew wrote his Gospel to the Hebrews in their own language.

The name of Matthew is the only one connected with our First Gospel by tradition, but there are several points of difficulty in the tradition. The earliest form of tradition, that of Papias, says that Matthew composed the "logia" in the "Hebrew dialect." By the Hebrew dialect he does not mean the classical Hebrew, the language of the Old Testament, but the Aramaic language, which was the language spoken by the Jews at that time. But does the word "logia," which means "oracles" or "sayings," have reference to our First Gospel in its present form? Can our First Gospel be considered a translation into Greek from an Aramaic original? A very few scholars think that all four of our gospels were originally written in Aramaic, but their views have found no general acceptance. The technique for the identification of translation Greek cannot be said to be perfected as yet, but some work has been done on it. In the Septuagint (the Greek Old Testament, often referred to by the symbol LXX), we have definite examples of Greek produced by translation from Semitic originals. The translations of these Old Testament books were made at various times by translators of varying ability. In some parts, the translation is so literal that the result is about as much Hebraic as Greek; in other parts, the Greek is very smooth. There is, of course, a bare possibility that the Gospel of Matthew may be a translation from an

Aramaic original, but it does not look like one. A theory of an Aramaic original of Matthew would necessitate quite a change in the accepted solutions of the synoptic problem also.

It is possible that by the "logia" Papias did not mean an original form of our present gospel, but a collection of the sayings of Jesus. Some have thought that our synoptic source "Q" may have been the Matthean logia, and that our Gospel got the name Matthew attached to it by reason of the fact that the logia played such a prominent part in the Gospel. "Q" was translated into Greek before it was incorporated into Matthew and Luke. It is possible that Matthew was responsible for "Q," possibly in Aramaic, and that he also had a connection with the composition of the gospel until it reached its final Greek form.

Papias may have been referring to our Gospel and have been mistaken, for some reason, about the Aramaic original. In some ways Matthew is the most Jewish of the gospels, and this fact may have caused the belief that it was written first in Aramaic.

Such is the state of confusion that exists. It must be acknowledged that we cannot be sure of the exact connection of Matthew with the Gospel that is known by his name. Matthew's name is the only one that tradition connects with the Gospel. His connection must have been closer than Peter's with the Second Gospel. Tradition has considered him the responsible guarantor of the contents of the Gospel.

Matthew, or Levi, the son of Alphaeus, was a tax-gatherer, working under the Roman government. These publicans were hated violently by the Jews for many reasons; the traditional association is "publicans and sinners." But Jesus said, "Follow me," and Matthew left his work and followed. Jesus chose him to be one of the twelve apostles. He gave a great feast for

Jesus and appeared in the first of Acts after the resurrection; apart from these facts the New Testament is silent about him. Tradition has very little to say about his later career. He is said to have labored in Ethiopia and around the Black Sea. Clement of Alexandria, about 200, quoted the Gnostic Heracleon to the effect that Matthew escaped martyrdom, but his martyrdom in Ethiopia is commemorated by both the Greek and Roman Catholic Churches.

Luke and Acts

It is necessary to discuss the authorship of these two books together, as they were written by the same person. The first verses in both books are introductions, and both introductions tell us that the books were written for the same person, Theophilus. The introduction of the Acts refers to the Gospel as: "The former treatise have I made, O Theophilus, of all that Jesus began both to do and teach, Until the day in which he was taken up." The style of the two books is the same also; the Greek is smooth and polished, much like the literary Greek of the Classical period. It is now a commonplace of New Testament criticism that the Third Gospel and the Book of Acts are volumes one and two of the same work. Who, then, was the author of this compound work?

He was one of Paul's companions on certain of his missionary journeys. We learn this from the "we-sections" of Acts, 16:10-17; 20:5 - 21:18, and 27:1 - 28:16, where the narrative tells of what "we" did rather than what "they" did. These sections include the second missionary journey from Troas to Philippi, the third missionary journey from Philippi to Jerusalem, and Paul's journey as a prisoner from Caesarea to Rome. Now by studying the Book of Acts and the salutations of the letters of Paul that were written during these periods, we are able to make a close estimate as to who this companion may have been. Only one known companion will fit, Luke.[15] This, of course, does not prove that Luke was the author, but at least this harmonizes well with the other points that we shall make. Some few have thought that the "we-sections" were not written by the author of Luke-Acts, but were sections from someone else's travel diary interpolated by the author into the larger work. But the style of the "we-sections" is exactly the same as that of the rest of the work, and it is almost unthinkable that the author should have adapted the style of this diary so perfectly to his own style and then have failed to change the "we's" to they's."

Back in 1882, Dr. Hobart wrote *The Medical Language of St. Luke*, in which he tried to prove that Luke and Acts are so full of technical medical words and expressions that only a physician could have written them, and he concluded that that physician was Luke, the "beloved physician" of Colossians 4: 14. For a time his conclusions were widely accepted. But then Dr. Cadbury wrote an article, *The Style and Literary Method of Luke*, in the *Harvard Theological Studies*, vi, i, completely wrecking Hobart's proof. Of Hobart's more than 400 "medical" terms, more than ninety percent were shown to be found in such non-medical literaature as Josephus and the Septuagint. Then, too, Hobart's standard, the physician Galen, states that he and his predecessor, Hippocrates, used terms that could be understood by the common people. It is really impossible to set up any standard for a technical medical vocabulary in the early days, even if we could assume that there was one. We cannot say now that the author of Luke-Acts must have been a physician, though he

[15] Certain scholars include Titus, but an early dating of Galatians excludes him.

may well have been one; Hobart's "proof" can now be considered little more than a suggestion.

Tradition tells us that the author of Luke-Acts, who was a companion of Paul, and who may have been a physician, was Luke the physician. Irenaeus, about 185, wrote: "And Luke, the follower of Paul, put in a book the gospel that was preached by him." The Muratorian Fragment, probably written in Italy between 170 and 200, said that the Third Gospel was written by Luke the physician, the companion of Paul. The early tradition is unanimously in favor of the Lukan authorship. If Luke did not write Luke-Acts, why would such a minor character have been chosen and held to so unanimously? It is the almost unanimous opinion of New Testament scholarship today that Luke was the author; the few who are still in doubt are not able to make any case for anyone else.

Luke is another one of the interesting and attractive minor characters of the New Testament. In Col. 4:14, "Luke, the beloved physician," joins Paul in sending greetings to the saints of Colossae. He is distinguished from Paul's Jewish companions in Col. 4:11, so he is the one Gentile who was inspired by God to write a book of the New Testament. In Philemon 24, Luke, as one of Paul's fellow-laborers, sends his greeting to Philemon. Luke was with Paul during his first imprisonment when he wrote these two letters. He was also with him during his later imprisonment; II Tim. 4:11 reads: "Only Luke is with me." Paul's other companions left him as the end approached, but the beloved physician was faithful. These are the only places in the New Testament where Luke is mentioned by name. The "we-sections" tell us something of his activity with Paul. Ramsey suggests that Luke may have been the man of Macedonia that called Paul to Europe, though tradition made him a native of Syrian

Antioch. While Paul was in prison for two years in Caesarea, Luke had a splendid opportunity of carrying on his research into the history of the life of Jesus and the early Church; though not an apostle himself, he was very close to them. He was a man of intelligence and culture, a man of science of his day. He wrote his two-volume work to "the most excellent Theophilus," and the Greek word translated "most excellent" was regularly used for the Roman nobility of the rank of Knight or above. We know nothing of the time or manner of Luke's death.

Dates of the Synoptics and Acts

The gospels tell us about the death of Jesus, so they could not have been written before about 30 A.D. Acts takes us to the Roman imprisonment of Paul, so about 61 is the earliest possible date to assign to it. When we come to the earliest part of the second century, we find all of these books being used, so they must have been written some time in the first century. These are rather wide limits. It is probable that some years elapsed after the death of Jesus before the Gospels were produced. Many were expecting His speedy return, but as that was delayed and His original followers began to die, it was deemed important that accurate memories of Jesus should be preserved. Probably the last half of the first century saw the production of the synoptics and Acts. Our study of the synoptic problem made us sure that Mark was the first Gospel written. Matthew and Luke seem to have been written about the same time, as neither one seems to have used the other. Acts was written to follow Luke. We can be rather sure of the relative order of our books, from Mark to Acts.

In general, there are two tendencies in the dating of these books. The earlier dating dates Acts at the time when Paul had been in prison two years, about 61; Luke and Matthew would be slightly earlier; and Mark would be even earlier, possibly around 50. The later dating dates Mark around 70 and the other books later, on down toward the close of the century.

Let us see some of the evidence in favor of the later dating.

Irenaeus[16] said that Mark wrote his gospel after the death (*exodos*) of Peter and Paul, which would put Mark too late to fit into the scheme for the earlier dating. But there are difficulties in connection with this testimony. The Greek word *exodos* may mean death and it may mean departure, though even the latter would not help much. But a more serious objection to Irenaeus' testimony is that he makes Matthew the first gospel instead of Mark; if we take his evidence too seriously, the whole solution to the synoptic problem will be destroyed. Then this Irenaeus passage contains that strange statement about Matthew's gospel being written in the language of the Hebrews. We must not put too much weight on a passage so full of difficulties. Irenaeus was thinking primarily about authorship.

Toward the close of His ministry, Jesus uttered a prophecy concerning the fall of Jerusalem and the end of the age, sometimes called "The Little Apocalypse." This is contained in the 13th of Mark, the 24th of Matthew, and Luke 21:5-38; there is also a short section, Luke 19:41-44. Now Radical criticism does not believe in the possibility of real predictive prophecy; a reputed prophecy is either a natural guess, or it is something written after the event and placed in the mouth of the reputed prophet. Especially in Matthew and Luke, the details of the destruction of

---

16 **Against Heresies, 3, 1, 1.**

Jerusalem are given too accurately to have been a guess, so the Radical says that these gospels were written after the destruction of Jerusalem (70 A.D.), that Jesus never spoke these words, but that they were written by His followers and put into His mouth as prophecy. Some Radicals think that Jesus may have guessed as accurately as the Markan form of the "prophecy," but some date even Mark after 70. If one holds to the Radical view of prophecy, it is necessary to take the later dating for the gospels, or at least use some subjective interpolation theory. A Conservative, who believes in the reality of predictive prophecy, is not moved by such an argument as this.

There are some who think that Luke made use of Josephus' *Antiquities* and *Jewish War*. If he did, he could not have written Luke and Acts before about 95. But this has been by no means proved, as is admitted by the most Radical. The case rests on the supposed use (or misuse) by Luke of information about Lysanias in Luke 3:1,[17] Theudas in Acts 5:36, 37,[18] and the Egyptian in Acts 21:37, 38.[19] This would be a strong point if it could be proved, but it cannot.

The general Radical approach almost demands a late date for these books. If one starts with a naturalistic Jesus, time is needed for the growth of the mythology about Him that is found in the gospels and for the growth of a Church as highly organized as that in the Book of Acts. The more time, the fewer difficulties. The old Tubingen school used to date some of the books down in the third century; that cannot be done now, but Radicals tend to date them as late in the first century as possible. The Conservative reconstruc-

[17] **Ant.** 18:6:10; 19:5:1; 20:7:1; 15:4:1; 15:10:1; **Jewish War** 1:22:3.

[18] **Ant.** 20:5:1f.

[19] **Jewish War** 2:13:3-5; **Ant.** 20:8:6.

tion does not need a late dating; in fact, the Conservative prefers an early date if the facts will allow one.

Luke said (1:1) that "many" had drawn up narratives before him. That is very indefinite; it may have been fulfilled by the year 60 as well as by the year 100.

Some think of the writing of Acts as the occasion of the collection of the Pauline letters and see a reflection of this in the letters to the Churches in Revelation and the collection of the Ignatian letters about 110. This is highly theoretical at best.

Let us see some of the reasons in favor of the earlier dating.

Acts ends very abruptly: "And Paul dwelt two whole years in his own hired house, and received all that came in unto him, preaching the kingdom of God, and teaching those things which concern the Lord Jesus Christ, with all confidence, no man forbidding him." Why did Luke stop just there? Why did he not tell about Paul's death, if that came next, or about his release and further work, if that followed? Probably the simplest explanation would be that Luke did not tell any more because no more had happened; Acts was published when Paul had been in prison two years in Rome, about 61. It may be that we have here the clue to the dating. But that is not the only explanation possible. It may be that Luke wrote, or planned to write, a third volume, telling the rest of the life of Paul; Acts 1:1 calls the Gospel "the first word," using the superlative rather than the comparative adjective. But "first" (protos) may be simply a numeral, or if it is a true superlative it need not demand more than two: and no one has ever heard of a third volume. It may be, however, that Acts did not originally end as it does now; Luke may have told more, and the ending may have been lost, as was the ending of Mark.

That is possible, though there is no textual evidence that such a thing happened for Acts, while there is abundant evidence that it happened for Mark. Or some other explanation may account for the abrupt ending of Acts.

When Luke tells about the prophecy of Agabus in Acts 11:28, he tells also about its fulfilment, because it was fulfilled before he wrote. But when he tells about Jesus' prophecy of the destruction of Jerusalem in the Little Apocalypse, he does not record its fulfilment. This suggests that Jerusalem had not been destroyed when the Gospel was written. We must avoid, however, putting too much weight on an argument from silence.

Some feel that the early date is preferable because Luke shows so little knowledge of the letters of Paul in the Acts. This, too, is an argument from silence.

We see that there is little of a definite nature to help us date our books. The Radical is almost compelled to take a late date by reasons which mean little or nothing to a Conservative. The Conservative realizes that there is nothing of great weight to force him either way; the most definite thing that he can see is that an early dating is probably the best explanation of the abrupt end of Acts. We may suggest very tentatively: Mark, about 50; Matthew and Luke, about 60; Acts, about 61.

VII

THE LIFE OF CHRIST

ALL four of the gospels have as their primary motive the telling of the story of Jesus in such a way that men will believe on Him and become Christians. Luke gives his purpose in his first four verses, that Theophilus might know the truth about the things of the faith in which he had been instructed. John tells us his purpose in 20:31: "But these are written that ye might believe that Jesus is the Christ, the Son of God; and that believing ye might have life through his name."

Men today are holding two general views of Jesus; some think of Him as only a man, while others think of Him as the God-man.

THE PURELY HUMAN JESUS

Many scholars start with a denial of the miraculous. Jesus, then, could have been only a man; He may be called divine only in the sense that all men are divine. The gospels are full of reputed miracles; therefore, these scholars cannot have a very high appreciation of the historicity of the sources of the life of Jesus. How can they trust sources that are so full of the unbelievable? What can they believe about Jesus? They must throw away large portions of the gospels; what can they hold?

They agree among themselves as to certain denials.

Jesus was not God incarnate. He did not work miracles. His death was not an atonement for the sins of others. He did not rise from the dead. He is not coming again. They agree among themselves that Jesus did live and that He was responsible for the rise of the Christian Church.[1] But agreement goes no further. Very few of them are content with such a faint picture of Jesus, yet none will take the complete picture of the gospels. Each one, then, takes from the sources just those elements that will fit into his own theoretical reconstruction of the life of Jesus. It is not surprising that there is the widest disagreement as to what Jesus did and said.

For some, Jesus was nothing more than a great teacher of morals—just another Plato or Epictetus. But what was the content of His teaching? How can we recover it from such imperfect sources? Synoptic criticism helps little; the sources of the gospels are under suspicion too, because they also are full of the miraculous. There is the widest disagreement, then, as to what Jesus did teach; some think of Him as the great pacifist; others, as the great socialist, or the great Rotarian, or the great ascetic. Most of these place a rather high value on the Sermon on the Mount, though only part of this can be considered as coming from an early source, Q.

Others say that Jesus did little or no teaching. He was a man who thought himself to be the Messiah. What kind of Messiah did he think himself to be? If he thought that he was a supernatural Messiah, he was, of course, wrong. If he expected to lead a political revolution against Rome, he was just another tragic failure

[1] The old Radical view that Jesus never lived at all is not in good repute even in the most Radical circles today. For a purely Radical defense of the historicity of Jesus see S. J. Case's **The Historicity of Jesus, 1912. Second edition, 1928.**

like so many others of that time. What did he expect the Kingdom of God to be? Is such a Kingdom ever to be established? What value does a Messianic Jesus have for us today? Again, one encounters widespread disagreement.

These scholars differ also as they face another vital problem. How can they account for the gospels in their present form if they start from any of the purely natural pictures of Jesus? They tend to date the gospels and their sources as late as possible and to allow their authors as little contact as possible with the actual life of Jesus; they want time for the alleged tradition to grow. As they conceive of the historic Jesus in so many different ways, their starting points are different, so they must use various routes to arrive at the same end, the Jesus of the gospels. One of the most complete hypothetical reconstructions of the growth of the tradition from the naturalistic Jesus is that found in Dean Case's *Jesus Through the Centuries.*[2] Let us review briefly the steps that he takes.

Case's Jesus was only a man who died a tragic death. After his death, his followers were discouraged, and the movement he started was about to die. But the movement took on new life when Peter and his friends got the idea that Jesus had risen from the dead. Case, as a historian, admits that Peter's assurance that he had seen Jesus alive after the crucifixion is one of the best-attested facts of ancient history.[3] Case does not believe that Jesus did rise, and he is honest enough to say that he does not know how the disciples came to hold that belief. After the belief got started, however, the disciples went everywhere preaching the new faith and winning new converts to the martyr who had triumphed over death. Soon the converts began to

[2] 1932, University of Chicago Press.
[3] P. 38.

think that their triumphant martyr was the Messiah and that he was coming again from heaven to set up his kingdom; they thought that Jerusalem would be the center of the kingdom, so they continued to work there and wait for his return. As the return was delayed and Christians had more contact with the Gentile world, it was natural that Jesus should be thought of as a hero who had been taken into the godhead after the fashion of many of the Greek and Roman heroes. After more contact with the heathen world, Jesus became the lord of the cult, in imitation of the various lords of the mystery cults of the day. Later, contact with the philosophies current resulted in the identification of Jesus with the divine *Logos*, and he became God incarnate. The next step was easy for Gentile Christians to take, that of identifying Jesus as Jehovah. Case also gives chapters tracing the growth after the time of the New Testament: "Jesus and Metaphysics," "The Jesus of Catholic Theology," "The Jesus of Medieval Piety," and "The Jesus of Protestantism."

These scholars must make some such reconstruction, starting, as they do, with a purely human Jesus. All of their findings are purely theoretical, however, and all of them have many gaps which no honest man can bridge save by an "I don't know." They must admit, also, that no one of their pictures of Jesus is the Jesus of historic Christianity; from the very earliest times Christians were convinced that Jesus was much more than a man. If one cannot believe in the miraculous, he must perforce adopt some form of this theory, but he must recognize that all such theories are fraught with difficulties, and that they are, at best, only theories. If he is consistent, he must be willing to go as far as Bultmann and say that we cannot now make out the character of Jesus, the vivid picture of His personality and life; and admit that it is impossible to produce positive evidence of the authenticity of a single word of Jesus.[4]

The Biblical Picture of Jesus

The Conservative admits the possibility of the miraculous; he believes that that is scientifically and philosophically possible. He applies the tests of historical science to the gospels and comes to have a high respect for their historicity. He has no *a priori* reasons for disbelieving the gospels, and the positive evidence leads him to believe that they paint a true picture of Jesus. After a study of all the competing theories, he comes to the conclusion that the best explanation of all the facts is that Jesus was what the gospels said that He was. The Conservatives reserve the right to apply the principles of historical criticism to every reputed event in the life of Christ, so there will be some variance among Conservatives; the differences, however, are very slight compared with the differences between those who believe in the naturalistic Jesus.

The Conservative admits that there are problems in the gospels. The gospel writers were not interested in many problems that interest modern historians. No one today can be sure of the exact date of the birth or the death of Jesus, though we know within a few years. No one can be sure as to the exact length of the public ministry or of the order of many of the events. We cannot be sure of the exact words that Jesus used in some of His sayings; different gospels give different words at times. The Conservative does not think that these problems are important enough to make him take the naturalistic alternative.

But far more important than these difficulties and

[4] **Form Criticism,** Bultmann and Kundsin, tr. by Grant, 1934, Willett, Clark, p. 61.

differences, Conservatives unite on what they consider the great positive certainties.

They have no difficulty in believing that Jesus was born as the gospels say, in a miraculous way, of a virgin and the Holy Spirit.[5] They believe that He was what the gospels repeatedly say that He was: the Messiah, the pre-existent *Logos*, the Son of God, God Himself, the God-man. They believe that He had the power of God at His command and that He did perform miraculous events as an expression of His love for needy men, a foretaste of the glories of the Kingdom, and a proof of His divinity. They believe that He was a great teacher; that He came to reveal to man God's way for the abundant life; they believe, also, that we have a true record of His teachings in the gospels. They believe that He came into the world to save the world; that His death was an atonement, not just a great tragedy; that through His death, man is freed once for all, when he believes, from the penalty of sin, and ever increasingly freed from the power of sin. They believe that He rose from the dead on the third day, validating all His claims, firing all His followers with zeal to preach His name to the ends of the earth. They believe that He is in glory now, and that He is coming again one day to set up His Kingdom in glory and to reign over the new heaven and the new earth with those who are His throughout eternity. Conservatives believe firmly that that is the true picture of the Jesus that lived; they know that that is the picture painted by the gospels, and that that is the faith that has inspired historic Christianity down through the centuries.

[5] Some few, like Brunner, believe in the true deity of Jesus without believing in the historicity of the Virgin Birth. The author believes that the Virgin Birth is true and is a very important doctrine, but he would not be inclined to make it an absolute **sine qua non** to Conservatism.

The Chronology of the Life of Christ

The birth of Jesus was not in the year A.D. 1. Dionysius Exiguus, in the sixth century, calculated when Jesus was born and used that as the starting point of the Christian era. But he made a mistake of several years. Herod the Great died 4 (possibly 3) B.C. But before he died, Jesus had been born, the Wise Men had told Herod but had not come back to him, Jesus and His family had left for Egypt, and Herod in his rage had ordered the slaughter of the infants two years old and under. The age of the infants does not necessarily push the birth of Jesus two years before the death of Herod. Herod died while they were in Egypt. We cannot be sure just when Jesus was born, but it was about 4-6 B.C.[6] We know nothing of the month or day of the month; the earliest information comes from about A.D. 200, when there were two traditions: in the East, Jan. 6; in the West, Dec. 25.

There is some uncertainty as to when Jesus began His public ministry. He was baptized by John, and Luke 3:1 dates the beginning of the ministry of John as the fifteenth year of Tiberius Caesar; but, unfortunately, we do not know whether Luke started counting from the death of Augustus or from some earlier time when Tiberius was associated with him. At the first passover of the ministry of Jesus, mentioned in John 2:20, it was said that the Temple had been in process of being built for forty-six years; but when was it started? Our information comes from Josephus, and it is rather confused, both as to the beginning of the reign of Herod and the year of the reign of Herod when the temple

---

[6] We get no help from the census mentioned in Luke 2:2, as that particular census is not mentioned elsewhere in literature; nor from the Fathers, as they all try to estimate from the death or baptism, and neither of those dates is certain, nor is the exact age of Jesus at either time certain.

was begun; a possible harmonizing of the difficulties makes the forty-sixth year of the Temple A.D. 27. Some authorities think that it is possible to date the fifteenth year of Tiberius as 25-26; if so, there is harmony between Luke and John, and we may date the baptism of Jesus sometime before the spring of 27.

How long did the public ministry last? There is nothing in the synoptic gospels to compel us to think that it lasted more than a year, though there is nothing to keep us from thinking that it may not have lasted longer. John, however, mentions several passovers, and they give us our best indication, though there are difficulties. It may not be necessary to assume that each passover is a different one; John may not have been trying to arrange his material chronologically. Or it may be that John did not mention all of the passovers that took place during the time of the ministry. Then we are not quite sure just how many passovers John does mention. One passover is mentioned in 2:13-23. 5:1 mentions "the feast of the Jews," which may or may not have been a passover, though some manuscripts omit the "the" and have simply "a feast of the Jews," which is most indefinite.[7] In 6:4 we find "the passover, the feast" mentioned, though there is a slight textual evidence that "the passover" should be omitted, which may then leave the feast a passover or not.[8] Then there is the passover of the crucifixion, mentioned in 11:55. Two, three, or four passovers are mentioned in John, then, depending on our views of the text and our interpretation. The minimum ministry in John would be something over a year and the maximum about four years, assuming that John mentioned all the passovers. The traditional estimate of about three years may be about right.

7 BDG and a few others omit "the."

8 Origen omits "the passover."

When was Jesus crucified? There are problems as to the hour, the day of the week, the day of the month, and the day of the year.

The synoptic gospels say that He was crucified at the third hour, or nine o'clock. In John 19:14, though, Jesus is still on trial at the sixth hour. There seems to be a contradiction. Some have solved the difficulty by supposing that John was using a different system of time, one like ours, so that the sixth hour was six o'clock. That would harmonize beautifully, but there is no evidence that such a method was in use at that time; John seems to use the regular method elsewhere in his gospel. Possibly in some early manuscript of John a six was confused with a three; that would be very easy with Greek numerals, a digamma (F) being confused with a gamma (Γ). If that be so, John's having Him on trial at the third hour and the synoptics' having Him on the cross at the third hour would be close enough, when we remember that they had no watches and that all the hours were given only approximately.

Jesus rose on "the third day," which was the first day of the week, Sunday. According to the ancient method of counting time, that makes the crucifixion to have taken place on Friday. From Friday to Sunday may even be called "after three days and three nights."

John seems to say that Jesus was crucified on the fourteenth of the month of Nisan, the day before the passover; while the synoptics seem to say the fifteenth, passover itself. Many articles and books have been written on this problem, and many theoretical harmonizations have been made, but we cannot go into them here.[9] Some think it was the fourteenth, and they find various ways of making the synoptics fit in with

[9] For a fuller discussion, see the dictionary articles and commentaries.

John; some do just the opposite. No one can be sure with the information that we have at present.

The year of the crucifixion is also in doubt. There is no certain way to compute it. We are not sure just when the ministry started and how long it lasted, so we cannot add those together with any certainty. We are not sure whether it was on the fourteenth or fifteenth of the month, so looking in the vicinity for a year when that date came on Friday will not give us any sure result; the astronomical methods of the Jews were so crude that we would get little help even if we could decide between the fourteenth and the fifteenth. The evidence of the Fathers helps little. Twenty-nine, thirty, and thirty-three are the dates most in favor, but we cannot be quite sure of any one of them.

A Suggested Outline of the Life of Christ

I. Birth and Childhood; Judaea, Egypt, Galilee:
Mt. 1:1 - 2:23; Mk. 1:1; Lk. 1:1 - 2:52.

II. Preparation and First Year; The Year of Obscurity; Judaea, Galilee, Samaria:
Mt. 3:1 - 4:11; Mk. 1:2-13; Lk. 3:1 - 4:13; Jn. 1:1 - 4:54.

III. Second Year; The Year of Popularity; Judaea, Galilee:
Mt. 4:12 - 14:36; Mk. 1:14 - 6:56; Lk. 4:14 - 9:17; Jn. 5:1 - 7:1.

IV. Third year; The Year of Opposition; Judaea, Galilee, Perea:
Mt. 15:1 - 20:34; Mk. 7:1 - 10:52; Lk. 9:18 - 19:28; Jn. 7:2 - 12:11.

V. The Last Days; Jerusalem:
Mt. 21:1 - 27:66; Mk. 11:1 - 15:47; Lk. 19:29 - 23:56; Jn. 12:12 - 19:42.

VI. The Resurrection and Ascension; Judaea, Galilee:
Mt. 28:1-15; Mk. 16:1-20; Lk. 24:1-53; Jn. 20:1 - 21:25

VIII

THE ACTS OF THE APOSTLES

We have already discussed the questions of authorship and date in connection with the synoptic gospels. It should be remembered that Acts is volume two of the work Luke-Acts.

The gospel of Luke told the story of the Founder of Christianity, from His birth until His ascension. The Book of Acts continues the story of the founding of Christianity, telling again the story of the ascension and of the giving of the Great Commission, and telling how the followers of Jesus carried out that Commission until finally the Gospel reached Rome itself.

There were four gospels, but there is only one Acts. Acts is the only book in the New Testament which gives us a narrative of those important first years in the development of the Christian Church from about 30 to 60. If it were not for Acts, we would have to reconstruct the picture from only the hints which come from some of the epistles. Acts, itself, gives us by no means a complete picture, but Luke has selected quite wisely a group of the most important events in connection with important churches and persons. The title suggests that we have a history of the acts of all the apostles, but such is not the case; the first part of Acts follows the life of Peter rather closely, and the last part, the life of Paul; other apostles play a small part.

Of course, Luke did not write the title himself. "The Acts of the Holy Spirit" has been suggested as probably a more appropriate title.

Luke almost certainly used sources for the composition of Acts as he did for his gospel. But we cannot determine at all accurately what those sources were, as there are no parallel Acts and none of the sources are still extant. The "we-sections"[1] indicate that Luke was with Paul on parts of his second and third journeys and his journey to Rome. Some of his material came from things that he had seen with his own eyes. His close friend, Paul, could easily supply information about his other acts. His being at Jerusalem, Caesarea, and Rome put him in a position to have contact with other leaders in the work of the church. His sources may have been entirely oral, though it has been suggested that he may have had access to some written sources from Jerusalem and Antioch, especially for the material in the first part of Acts.

Whatever the sources may have been, Luke seems to have produced a work of high historical reliability. Of course he does not tell us many things that modern historians consider important, especially about chronology; but what he does tell us meets the tests of historicity. Time and again Luke has been accused of inaccuracy, but a fuller discovery of the facts has shown that the truth was with him rather than with his critics. A few historical problems remain, but we are at least safe in giving Luke the benefit of the doubt while waiting for further light. Luke seems to have made little or no use of the letters which Paul had written, but Acts and the epistles are in beautiful harmony. Luke knows his geography and his political history well. Whenever we can test Luke's accuracy,

[1] Acts 16:10-17; 20:5 - 21:18; 27:1 - 28:16.

it stands the test; we feel justified, then, in assuming that he is also habitually accurate.

Luke wrote Luke-Acts so that Theophilus might know the truth about Christianity. Some think that Theophilus is a name for the Christian in general, "Lover of God"; but probably it was the name of an actual person, a Roman nobleman. The Greek word translated "most excellent" was regularly used for Roman nobility of the equestrian rank. Some have thought that Luke wrote Luke-Acts so as to obtain the help of this Roman nobleman in having Paul released from prison. An early dating allows this as a possibility. But then, Luke's primary interest may have been historical and doctrinal. Theophilus may have been one who was thinking of becoming a Christian, or he may have been a Christian who was interested in knowing more about the Founder and the development of the Church. At any rate, Acts is for us today a most valuable source of information about the growth of our Church in its formative years.

An Outline of the Contents

I. *The Church in Jerusalem,* 1:1 - 8:3. Jesus gives His parting instructions to His disciples. They waited, as he directed, in prayer, until the Holy Spirit was poured out in power on the day of Pentecost. Three thousand came into the Church in one day, and soon the number had grown to five thousand. The early Christian life was characterized by bravery, love, and sharing. The Christians continued to worship in the temple, and they used it as a place to preach Jesus and work miracles in His name, though it got them into trouble with the Jewish authorities. Finally the opposition resulted in actual persecution; Stephen, the first Christian martyr, was stoned, and persecution broke out with such force that Christians were driven out of Jerusalem into the surrounding country.

II. *The Church in Judaea and Samaria,* 8:4 - 12:25. The persecuted Christians took their message with them, even to the hated Samaritans. While preaching with great success but incurring opposition. They retrace Spirit down to the Gaza road to lead the Ethiopian eunuch to Christ. The persecutor Saul sees a vision of the risen Christ on the road to Damascus and becomes a member of the group that he had been trying to exterminate. After the vision of the sheet let down from heaven, Peter carries the gospel to the Gentile army officer, Cornelius; the Jewish Christians had their doubts about this step, but they finally gave their approval to it. The persecuted Christians go as far as Antioch, and a flourishing Church is soon in existence there. Barnabas is sent to Antioch from Jerusalem; he gets Saul from Tarsus, and they stay there for about a year. Herod joins in with the persecution in Jerusalem; he kills James, the brother of John, and puts Peter in prison, but Peter is miraculously delivered. Soon the persecutor died, "but the word of God grew and multiplied."

III. *The Church to the Uttermost Parts of the Earth,* 13:1 - 28:31.

A. The First Missionary Journey, 13:1 - 15:35. Barnabas, Paul and the young John Mark are sent out from Antioch. They sail to Cyprus and work their way through the island from east to west, winning, among others, the Roman deputy, Sergius Paulus. Then they sail north to the mainland of Asia Minor, landing at Perga; here Mark leaves them and goes back to Jerusalem. They go on inland and visit Pisidian Antioch, Iconium, Lystra, and Derbe, preaching with great success to the Samaritans, Philip was sent by the their steps as far as Perga and then sail back to Antioch in Syria. A controversy had arisen as to whether they had done right in taking Gentiles into the Church without circumcision, so Paul and Barnabas and others went to Jerusalem and put the question up to the Christian leaders there. The decision was rendered in favor of Paul's view, and Gentile Christianity steadily grew. They returned to Antioch.

B. The Second Missionary Journey, 15:36 - 18:22. Paul and Barnabas separate over the question of giving Mark a second chance. Barnabas takes Mark and goes to Cyprus. Paul takes Silas and goes overland to revisit those churches in southern Galatia that he had founded on the first journey. Being forbidden to enter the province of Asia or Bithynia, they come to Troas. There Paul sees the vision of the man of Macedonia, so they cross the Aegean Sea into Europe. They work their way south from Philippi down through Amphipolis, Apollonia, Thessalonica, Berea, and Athens to Corinth, where they stayed a year and a half. Then they sailed by Ephesus to Caesarea. Paul went up to salute the Church, probably at Jerusalem, and then went back to Antioch.

C. The Third Missionary Journey, 18:23 - 21:16. Paul revisits the Galatian churches and goes to Ephesus, where he stays three years. Then he goes to Troas and into Macedonia and Greece, revisiting the churches founded on the second journey and taking up a collection for the Church at Jerusalem. A plot against his life kept him from sailing directly to Jerusalem from Corinth, so he went back up to Philippi, sailed by way of Troas and Miletus to Tyre, and then went by land on up to Jerusalem, though he was repeatedly warned that he was taking his life in his hands.

D. Paul a Prisoner; Jerusalem, Caesarea, Rome; 21:17 - 28:31. At Jerusalem, the former persecutor received some of his own medicine. The Roman army rescued him from the mob and held him in prison for a trial. He was taken to Caesarea for safe keeping, where he was held for two years. Paul despaired of justice at the hands of Felix, Festus, and Agrippa, so he appealed to Caesar. After the shipwreck, he reached Rome. There as a prisoner, though in his own hired house, he preached the gospel for two years.

The Book of Acts ends thus abruptly. If Paul wrote the Pastoral Epistles, and there is good reason for thinking that he did, he was released from this first Roman imprisonment, made further journeys, and was imprisoned again. Tradition tells us that he met a martyr's death under Nero.

The Chronology of the Life of Paul

The Book of Acts gives us most of our information on this subject, which is necessary for the dating of the Pauline epistles. Here, as elsewhere in the New Testament, our information is not as full as we could desire. The meager chronological data of Acts make it possible for us to reconstruct a fairly definite schedule for the missionary journeys; Galatians is our best help for dating the earlier part of his life.

Until 1908, there was no fixed point in secular history that exactly corresponded with a fixed point in the life of Paul, so all dates had to be given very tentatively. But in that year, the Palestinian Exploration Fund described four broken pieces of stone which, when put together, proved to be parts of an imperial letter of the time of Claudius. On the pieces appear the name and titles of Claudius; the date, his twenty-sixth acclamation as emperor; the name Gallio; and the title proconsul. We are able, then, to date the proconsulship of Gallio at Corinth from the summer of 51 to the summer of 52. But Paul left Corinth on his second journey shortly after Gallio became proconsul; he had stayed there eighteen months, so he must have reached Corinth at the end of 49 or the beginning of 50. This gives us a rather definite fixed point right in the midst of Paul's missionary activity; from it we can work backward and forward with a fair degree of accuracy, using the older, less accurate fixed points as checks.

The Council of Jerusalem of Acts 15 can be dated about 48. Galatians 1:15 - 2:1 gives us Paul's own story of his life from his conversion until a trip to Jerusalem which most scholars identify with the Council trip of Acts 15. After his conversion he went to Arabia and returned to Damascus. After three years he went to Jerusalem. After fourteen years he went again to Jerusalem. There are still problems, however. Some identify the visit of Gal. 2:1 with the famine visit of Acts 11:30 - 12:25 instead of with the Council visit. Then again, do the fourteen years include the three years, or are they to be added together? Do the three years include the trip to Arabia or not? Then we must remember that the ancients counted a part of a year as a year. The minimum time between the Council and the conversion would be twelve years, plus two part years; the maximum, seventeen years, plus an unknown stay in Arabia; his conversion could be dated before 31 or down to 36. Or, if Gal. 2:1 is identified with Acts 11:30, we could push these dates back two or three years more. We know that Paul was not converted before the crucifixion of Jesus, but we cannot be sure of the date between then and about 36. The little chronological hints in Acts fitted into this brief outline make it possible for us to suggest the following dates as approximately correct:

33 —Conversion;
35 —Famine Visit to Jerusalem;
46-48—First Missionary Journey;

48 —Jerusalem Council;
49-52—Second Missionary Journey;
52-56—Third Missionary Journey;
56-58—Jerusalem and Caesarea;
59-61—First Roman Imprisonment;
67. —Martyrdom.

IX

THE PAULINE EPISTLES

It is not possible to be entirely certain as to the chronological order of these epistles, but we shall follow an order that presents at least a possible chronology. The Epistle to the Hebrews is sometimes included in this group, but it will be discussed separately.

The Epistle to the Galatians

The Destination. This Epistle is addressed to "the Churches of Galatia," but there is a question as to what is meant by "Galatia." In the third century B.C., large numbers of the Gauls migrated from Eastern Europe to a district in the North of central Asia Minor, and that district became known as Galatia. Pessinus, Ancyra, and Tavium were the chief cities. When Rome became a world empire, the territory was divided into provinces for purposes of administration. The Roman province of Galatia included the district where the Galatians lived, but it also included the districts south of it, Lycaonia, Pisidia, and Phrygia, right down to the Mediterranean. The Roman province of Galatia included those cities that Paul visited on his first missionary journey, Derbe, Lystra, Iconium, and Antioch.

Because of these two uses of the word Galatia, two theories have arisen as to the destination of the Epistle. The North Galatian theory is that the letter was written to the Churches in the district settled by the Gauls, ethnic Galatia, which Paul had founded on his second missionary journey, Acts 16:6. The South Galatian theory is that Galatia means the Roman province of Galatia, and that the churches addressed were those in the southern part, Derbe, Lystra, Iconium, and Antioch, which Paul founded on his first journey, Acts 13-14. Both of these theories are still in good repute; after weighing the evidence each person may follow the theory that seems more probable to him. These theories play a large part in the dating of the Epistle, so it will be necessary for us to consider something of the evidence.

The North Galatianists claim that people writing of territory that was thoroughly familiar to them would naturally use the popular rather than the technical terms for it; possibly so, but we cannot be sure that the northern sense was any more popular than the southern. Then Luke, in Acts, regularly uses geographical names without any political significance, such as Mysia, Phrygia, and Pisidia; but we must remember that we are primarily interested in Paul's usage rather than Luke's, and even Luke uses Asia in its political sense. Luke actually calls Lystra and Derbe cities of Lycaonia and Antioch a city of Pisidia; but again this is Luke's usage; and then the fact that Atlanta is in Georgia does not prove that it is not also in the United States. The North Galatianists also ask: If the letter was sent to the churches founded on the first journey, why does not Acts tell us about Paul's sickness mentioned in Gal. 4:13, and why does not Galatians tell us about some of the persecution which is so prominent in Acts 13-14? This is an argument from silence, which can never conclusively prove anything; the argument is not very strong when we remember how brief both accounts are, in Galatians and Acts.

The South Galatianists marshal quite an array of arguments. Paul regularly, if not exclusively, uses terms in their official, Roman sense, such as the Roman provinces of Judaea, Syria, Cilicia, Asia, Macedonia, and Achaia; there is a strong probability, then, that he uses Galatia in that same sense. In Galatians, Paul gives details of his Christian life, but he stops (Gal. 2:11) when Peter came to Antioch before the second journey; on the Southern theory we can explain this by dating the Epistle at this time and saying that nothing more had happened; on the Northern theory there is an inexplicable gap. In Acts 15 the controversy over circumcision took place at the Jerusalem Council, and there is no indication that the controversy ever broke out again; the Southern theory can date the Epistle early and make it fit into this background; the Northern theory must date the Epistle later and must assume that the controversy broke out again after having been once settled, which is possible but not probable. Possibly even Acts uses Galatia in the provincial sense, so that the expression "the Galatian and Phrygian country" (Acts 16:6 and 18:23) may mean that part of Phrygia which was in the Roman province of Galatia. Then there is no mention of the founding of any churches in the Galatia of Acts 16 and 18; the statement is simply that he "passed through" these regions; and not one of the cities in Northern Galatia is mentioned in the New Testament. The note in Gal. 4:14, "Ye received me as an angel," looks very much like the reception at Lystra in Acts 14:12, where Barnabas is called Zeus and Paul, Hermes, the messenger or angel of the gods. In Acts 20:4, there is a list of delegates chosen to take the collection back with Paul; there is no delegate from North Galatia but two, Gaius and Timothy, from cities in South Galatia. In Gal. 2:1, 13, Paul mentions Barnabas; Barnabas was well-known to the cities in the South, because he was with Paul on the first journey; he did not go with Paul on the second or third journey. It is easier to see why the Judaizers from Jerusalem went to the more accessible cities of the South than to the far-away cities of the North. In Gal. 4:13, Paul says that he preached to them because of sickness; the South Galatianists can give a probable reconstruction of this by assuming that he left the swampy lands of the Mediterranean coast and went just north into the mountains of South Galatia; the North Galatianist does not have his swamps and mountains so close together, but he, too, can take care of this. In Gal. 1:6, Paul marvels that the Galatians are removing from the true gospel "so quickly"; the South Galatian theory makes an earlier dating possible, thereby making the "so quickly" a little quicker than is possible on the other theory.

No one of the reasons alleged on either side is quite conclusive; many of them are quite weak. The balance of probability seems to be somewhat in favor of the South Galatian theory.[1]

The Date

Gal. 4:13 says: "Ye know how through infirmity of the flesh I preached the gospel unto you at the first." The Greek words translated "at the first" mean literally "the former time," implying, though not absolutely proving, that Paul had made two visits to them before he wrote the Epistle. On the North Galatian theory, the first visit would have been on the second missionary journey (Acts 16:6), and the second visit on the third journey (Acts 18:23). The Epistle could not have

[1] For a fuller discussion of these theories, see E. D. Burton, **Galatians**, in I. C. C., pp. xxi ff (Southern), and J. B. Lightfoot, **Galatians**, pp. 1 ff (Northern), and J. Moffatt, **Introduction to the Literature of the N. T.**, pp. 90 ff (Northern).

been written, then, until late on the third journey, the most probable places being Ephesus or Corinth. This would make Galatians one of the later epistles, written about the same time as the Corinthian Epistles and Romans. On the South Galatian theory, the first visit would have been on the first missionary journey, and the second visit could have been on the same journey, because after visiting the cities once, he revisited them. The earliest possible dating, then, would be just after the first missionary journey. Other South Galatianists think that the second visit was on the second journey, so they date it somewhat later. Others think that he may have visited them more than twice, so they date it as late as the North Galatianists.

Gal. 2:1-10 tells about a visit of Paul to Jerusalem to discuss the problem of circumcision and Gentile Christianity. Most interpreters think that that is the same visit that is mentioned in Acts 15, the Jerusalem Council visit, which took place between the first and second missionary journeys.[2] If so, the Epistle could not have been written until after the Council; it may have been written at Antioch in Syria just before the second journey. If, however, the Gal. 2 visit is identified with the Acts 11:30 visit, the famine visit, it is most probable that Galatians was written at Antioch just after the first journey, just before the Jerusalem Council.

Is it possible to choose between these possibilities? The North Galatianists and some of the South Galatianists favor a later dating because of the similarity of style between Galatians and Corinthians and Romans. It is true that the great theme of all of these epistles is justification by faith, but that is no proof

[2] There is a difference in emphasis in Acts and Galatians, but the similarities seem stronger than the apparent differences. See the commentaries for a fuller discussion of this point.

that they were all written at about the same time. That was the major theme in Paul's theology, and he could emphasize it whenever the occasion demanded. And an argument from mere literary style is most precarious and proves little, if anything. An early dating has this great advantage: it is possible to date the Epistle in connection with the Jerusalem Council and think of the great controversy over circumcision as having broken out and having been settled once and for all. A later dating must suppose that it was settled once by the Council and that it broke out again to be settled by Paul in Galatians, which is, of course, possible but not so probable.

It is impossible to be absolutely certain about the date of the Epistle, but dating it at Antioch just after the Council, before the second journey, seems to meet the requirements best. This would make it the earliest of the Pauline epistles, and make the date about 48 A.D. Other possible dates, as we have seen, are: Antioch, just before the Council, about 48; Corinth, on the second journey, about 50; Ephesus, on the third journey, about 53-55; or Corinth, on the third journey, about 55-56. Soon after that we reach the prison epistles and Galatians does not belong to them.

The Occasion

The Galatians were nearly all, if not all, Gentiles. When Paul preached to them, he preached that they could be saved simply by believing in Jesus Christ. Many of the Galatians had become Christians on that basis, and churches had been established. However, this did not satisfy some of the stricter Jewish Christians, who thought that a person must become a Jew before he could become a Christian. To become a Jew, a man had to submit to the rite of circumcision and undertake to keep the Mosaic law, ritual as well as moral. These requirements had always kept Judaism from winning many converts; they usually meant that a person meeting them had to make a complete break with his past, religiously, socially, and economically. Now some of these stricter Jewish Christians, or Judaizers, went to the churches that Paul had founded in Galatia and told them that their faith was not a valid one, that Paul's gospel was a letting down of the bars, and that Paul himself was not a true apostle, that he had no authority to preach this new gospel of his. Naturally, the Galatians were greatly worried, and many of them were considering circumcision and the keeping of the law. They hardly knew what to think of Paul.

This was one of the great crises in the history of the Church, and Paul saw clearly the issues involved. The Jerusalem Council of Acts 15 shows the discussion of this problem by the whole Church and shows how Paul and his party convinced them. Paul cannot get to Galatia himself immediately, so he writes the Epistle. The Galatians, as all others, must choose between two ways of salvation, by keeping the law or by faith in Jesus Christ. To follow the teachings of the Judaizers meant that they were not trusting Jesus for salvation. Paul gives a ringing challenge to them to hold fast to the only true gospel—salvation, not by works, but by faith in the Lord Jesus Christ. This Epistle gave a vital message to the first century and had a large part in establishing historic Christianity on a solid foundation; it had a large part in reestablishing the true Church at the Reformation; it still has a vital, much-needed message for today.

The Contents

I. *Introduction, 1:1-5.* Paul and the brethren send greetings to the Churches of Galatia.

II. *Paul's apostolic authority vindicated, 1:6 - 2:21.* Paul is not thinking of his own glory, but he must defend his gospel by defending the truth and authority of its bearer. There is only one true gospel, the one he brought them. Paul's commission came not from men but from God. He had little contact with those who had been apostles before him, though they recognized him and approved of his gospel. Paul is so sure of the truth of his message that he could rebuke even Peter when Peter failed to act in accordance with it.

III. *Salvation is by faith, not by law, 3:1 - 5:6.* For the truth of this, Paul first appeals to the experience of the Galatians; did they receive the great spiritual gifts by keeping the law or by faith in Jesus? He then shows from the Old Testament that salvation has always been by faith rather than by works, even in the case of Abraham, the father of the Jews. He shows that it is unreasonable to think that the law of Moses would abrogate the covenant of faith made with Abraham four hundred years before Moses; even men's agreements are not broken in that way. The great purpose of the law was not to provide salvation, but to convince man of his need of salvation and guide him to the Savior, like the Greek slave, the pedagogue. Faith made the Galatians sons of God; after having made such a noble beginning, a return to the slavery of the law would be a senseless anti-climax. The Galatians had shown signs of an earnest Christian life, but now Paul is worried lest these signs may have been wrong and his work with them may have been in vain. He gives the illustration of Abraham's two sons and urges the Galatians to be like Isaac, the child of promise. The Galatians must choose between legalism and Christ.

IV. *Practical exhortations, 5:7 - 6:10.* As born by

the Spirit, the Galatians should bear the fruits of the Spirit. Good works are not the basis of salvation but the fruits. The Christian is no longer under the power of the flesh but of the Spirit.

V. *Conclusion, 6:11-18.* Paul takes the pen from the scribe, repeats some of the most important parts for emphasis, and autographs the letter.

First Thessalonians

Acts 17:1-10 tells how Paul preached in the Macedonian city of Thessalonica on his second missionary journey. After starting a church and preaching for some time, the Jews rose against him and created such a tumult that it was thought best for him to leave the city. He went on to Berea. The Thessalonian Jews followed him and created another disturbance there, so Paul left and went on to Athens, leaving Silas and Timothy in Macedonia. After his experience on the Hill of Ares in Athens, Paul went on down to Corinth. I Thess. 3:1 ff tells that he sent Timothy back to Thessalonica to establish the Christians and bring him news of them. From Acts 18:5, we learn that Timothy and Silas rejoined the Apostle at Corinth. It was in answer to the news brought by Timothy that Paul wrote I Thessalonians. This reconstruction allows us to be very sure about the place and date of writing, Corinth, on the second missionary journey, and almost certainly in the year 50 A.D. The most certain date in Pauline chronology is 50-51 for this stay of his in Corinth.

The news that Timothy had brought from Thessalonica was good, and the Apostle commends them highly for their fidelity in the face of hardships. But they needed instruction on certain points; one problem especially was giving them grave concern. They were expecting the speedy return of the Lord to set up His kingdom, but while He was delaying some of their number were dying; they were afraid that their dead friends would miss some of the glories of the kingdom. Paul tells them that those who die in Christ would miss nothing, but that when He comes they will rise first; then those that are alive will be caught up to be with them. The epistle is a reassurance, a commendation, and a little guide for Christian living in the midst of a pagan world. It contains the things that Paul would have said to them if he had been able to pay them a pastoral visit.

An Outline of the Contents

I. *Commendation, 1:1 - 3:13.* Paul praises the members of the Church and thanks God for their sincerity and fidelity, even in the face of persecution. He also recounts some of the history of his life while he was with them and after he had left, showing his own interest and earnestness toward them.

II. *Instruction, 4:1 - 5:28.* He beseeches them to go on nearer to perfection in morals—to be careful to avoid sexual irregularities and dishonesty, and to increase in love and industriousness. He gives them some instruction about the resurrection and the second coming of the Lord. The dead believers are to rise, and afterward the living believers are to be caught up to be with them and with Christ. But no man knows when all this is to happen. He exhorts the children of the light to live worthily, abstaining from all appearance of evil.

Second Thessalonians

The First Epistle had corrected the misunderstanding about those who died before the Second Coming, but Paul hears in some way they are still having trouble growing out of their expectation of a speedy return of the Lord. We do not know how they got the assurance that Jesus would return soon; it may have been a pure guess; it may have come from a misinterpretation of something that Paul had said; 2:2 suggests that it may have come from a letter that someone had sent them in the name of Paul. But, however they got the idea, they had no right to have it. Some of the Thessalonians had even stopped working—"No use to work and plan for the future if our Lord is coming back right away." Paul saw the danger of such an attitude, so he immediately sent this Second Epistle to them. "You must not believe that our Lord must come back immediately. Haven't I told you that before He comes there must be a falling away and the revelation of the man of sin? And as for those of your number who have stopped work in anticipation of His coming, if they won't work don't let them eat; maybe they will change their minds soon."

Silas and Timothy are still associated with Paul in the salutation. The whole situation seems much the same as it was in the First Epistle. It seems rather clear that the Second Epistle, too, was written at Corinth on the second missionary journey, probably not long after the First, in 50 or 51 A.D.

Some few scholars doubt the Pauline authorship of II Thessalonians because of the rather strange section about the man of sin primarily, but most believe that the negative reasons are nothing like as strong as the positive—the claims of the Epistle itself, the unanimous tradition, and its harmony with what we know of Paul and the Thessalonians.

An Outline of the Contents

I. *Commendation, 1:1-12.* As in the First Epistle, Paul thanks God for their fidelity under trying circumstances.

II. *Instruction about the Second Coming, 2:1-17.*

They should not believe that He must come speedily. No one knows when He is to come. The falling away and the man of sin are to come first, and Paul implies that they had not come at that time. Be ready for the Second Coming whenever it may come, not by stopping work, but by standing fast in all the truth of the gospel, by doing the things that will be pleasing to the Lord when He comes.

III. *Exhortations, 3:1-17.* Pray for Paul. Avoid those who walk disorderly. Don't be busybodies, but workers; no work, no food. Be not weary in well-doing. Farewell.

The Corinthian Correspondence

Corinth was a great city of southern Greece. It was an old city, but in 146 B.C. the Romans burned it because of rebellion. Its geographical location was so strategic for commercial purposes, however, that Julius Caesar rebuilt the city shortly before his death in 44 B.C. The population was made up largely of traders, many of them being freed slaves. Corinth contained many of the pagan cults of the day. These cults had their good features but also their bad ones. Reproduction in nature and in mankind played a large part, so that frequently immorality was carried on in the name of religion. Drunkenness and frenzy characterized many of the religious activities of some of the cults. The Graeco-Roman religion, with its polytheism, played its part. The patron deity of Corinth was Aphrodite, the goddess of love. In the old Corinth there had been a magnificent temple of Aphrodite with a thousand priestesses, little better than women of the street; probably the same thing was going on in the new Corinth. The Corinthians were so famous for their immorality that the Greeks coined a word, "Corinthianize," meaning "to act immorally." Those who became Christians had to live in the midst of a city that was anything but Christian; they were "called to be saints" even so. But the pagan atmosphere caused many problems for the young Christian Church there. First Corinthians, especially, gives us a vivid picture of the problems which they had to face.

Paul came to Corinth from Athens on his second missionary journey. Acts 18:1-18 tells us of his work there. He stayed eighteen months, probably from the winter of 49-50 to the summer of 51. He founded the Church there and stayed until the Jews ran him out.

Two letters from Paul to the Church of Corinth have been preserved in our New Testament, but other letters passed back and forth between them. Let us try to reconstruct the whole correspondence as fully as we can.

1. The Pre-Corinthian letter. Paul, in I Cor. 5:9, mentions that he had written to the Corinthians, urging them to refrain from association with fornicators. We do not know what else this letter contained or just when it was written. This letter was not preserved for our New Testament canon. There are some few scholars who do not believe in the unity of II Corinthians who believe that this letter is II Cor. 6:14 - 7:1; the subject-matter is somewhat the same, but we shall try to show later that the reasons for splitting II Corinthians into several letters are inconclusive.

2. A letter from Corinth to Paul. This letter is mentioned in I Cor. 7:1. The Corinthians write Paul for advice on some problems that were before them. This letter is not preserved, but we can get a good idea of the questions asked by the answers that Paul gave in I Corinthians, especially from 7:1 to the end. This letter came to Paul while he was in Ephesus on his third missionary journey.

As Ephesus was just across the Aegean Sea from

Corinth, Paul got reports from Corinth from time to time. In I Cor. 1:11 he mentions a report that he had received from some of the household of Chloe about factions in the Church. I Cor. 5:1 mentions a report of immorality, but whether it came from those of the household of Chloe or not we do not know.

3. *First Corinthians.* The reports and the letter showed Paul that the Corinthians needed help, so he writes our First Corinthians to them, dealing with the problems raised. From I Cor. 16:1-9, we learn that Paul wrote this letter from Ephesus on his third missionary journey, toward the close of his three-year stay there, probably about 55 A.D. He plans to stay on there through Pentecost and then come to Corinth by way of Macedonia. Timothy has been sent on ahead, also by way of Macedonia (Acts 19:22); Paul expects his letter to reach Corinth first, as it goes straight across the Sea.

If we put II Cor. 2:1, 12:14, and 13:1 together, we learn that Paul paid a visit to Corinth that is not recorded in Acts. Paul learns somehow that a crisis has arisen in the Church of Corinth. The trouble may have been with the factions or with the immorality mentioned in I Corinthians, but we cannot be sure. It was such a severe crisis, however, that Paul paid a visit to them and was with them in great sorrow.

4. *The rebuking letter.* Evidently Paul's visit did not solve the problem. Instead of visiting them again at this time, he writes them a sorrowful, rebuking letter, mentioned in II Cor. 2:1-11 and 7:8. This letter is probably not preserved, though some few think that it is II Cor. 10:1 - 13:14. It was written from Ephesus not long after I Corinthians, probably about 55 A.D. It may have been sent by Titus; at any rate, Titus was sent about this time to see what he could do with the problem (II Cor. 7, 8).

5. *Second Corinthians.* After Paul had sent the rebuking letter and Titus to Corinth, he left Ephesus for Troas, hoping to meet Titus there and hear good news from Corinth. But II Cor. 2:12, 13 tells us that Titus was not there, so Paul had to go on to Macedonia with a heavy heart. But somewhere in Macedonia Titus meets him with good news. Paul's heart is filled with joy that the crisis has been safely passed, so he immediately sends our Second Corinthians as a letter of reconciliation. He wanted this letter to get to Corinth even sooner than he could get there himself. It was written, probably, towards the end of 55 or the beginning of 56 A.D.

Acts 20:1-3 tells us that Paul spent three months in Greece on his third missionary journey, and the introduction to Romans proves that he was in Corinth. So he was able to make this third visit to a Church that was at peace again.

The Unity of Second Corinthians

There are some who think that our Second Corinthians is not one letter but a group of letters; several letters have been put together, and the introduction of the first and the conclusion of the last serve as the introduction and conclusion of the group. Some say that II Cor. 6:14 - 7:1 is the Pre-Corinthian letter. II Cor. 10 - 13 is sometimes considered the rebuking letter. Some even separate II Cor. 8 - 9 into one or two more letters, written after II Corinthians, before Paul reaches Corinth, urging the necessity of a good collection. After each scholar makes all the subtractions that seem necessary to him, what is left is II Corinthians, the letter of reconciliation.

It is true that these parts of II Corinthians are somewhat like the lost letters, but we need not assume that Paul treated such important matters only once; it is reasonable to suppose that Paul would mention again matters that were important enough to provoke such a crisis. It is true, also, that it is not always easy to follow Paul's train of thought from section to section, but that does not make it necessary to think that the different sections were different letters; Paul's mind jumps from subject to subject very rapidly even under normal circumstances; is it unreasonable to suppose that it would do so here after the anguish of the crisis and the thrill of the good news? The crisis has passed, but Paul harks back to it from time to time to warn them against a repetition. If II Corinthians is a unity, it gives us a splendid psychological picture of the working of Paul's mind in a time of great excitement.

Those who wish to split up the Epistle can point to no external evidence whatever. No single manuscript or patristic mention gives any justification.

Conservative critics tend to uphold the unity of the books as they stand. If several letters could have been jumbled into one letter, we cannot have a very high regard for the accuracy of what we have; our view of inspiration would have to be lowered a bit. If anyone can prove that some of our books are not units, we must be willing to admit the proof and make whatever adjustments are necessary. But we insist on strong proof. Most conservatives believe that the proof offered against the unity of II Corinthians is entirely too subjective and weak in general, and many critics of other schools join with them.

An Outline of First Corinthians

I. *Church factions, 1 - 4.* After an introduction, Paul goes immediately to the grave problem of divisions in the Church. Those from Chloe had told Paul that there were some who claimed to belong to Paul's party, some to Peter's, some to Apollos', and some to Jesus'.

Church splits are not the exclusive property of the twentieth century. But whenever they occur, they are wrong. All Christians are Christ's, and Christ is not divided. Paul and Peter and Apollos were simply servants of Christ. Paul and Apollos could plant and water, but God had to give the increase. Paul pleads for the true unity of the Church as the temple of God, in which the one Spirit of God dwells.

II. *Church discipline, 5 - 6.* Christians should be different from the world. When Church members commit gross sins, the Church must use discipline. Try to correct the sinner, but if that cannot be done, the purity of the Church must be protected. Then Paul urges the Christians to settle their differences among themselves and refrain from carrying them before pagan courts.

III. *Marriage and divorce, 7.* This is a long, difficult chapter. In its interpretation we must remember that Paul was dealing with a missionary problem. A man and a woman would be married before either ever heard of Christianity; one becomes a Christian, but the other refuses; what is to be done? If the unbeliever is willing to stay with the believer, let the marriage continue; if not, the believer can only let the unbeliever go. Marriage in pagan Corinth had its difficulties for Christians; under those trying conditions, it was sometimes best to refrain from marriage entirely. We are not justified in taking Paul's advice to these Corinthians out of its context and making it of immediate, universal application. We must try to separate between eternal principles and the temporary application of those principles; this is a difficult but necessary task of the interpreter.

IV. *Pagan contacts, 8 - 10.* The Corinthian Christians lived in the midst of a pagan city and had many contacts with paganism. What, for example, should they do about eating meat that had been offered to idols? Really an idol was nothing, and meat that had been offered to an idol was just as good as any other meat; there was nothing really wrong in eating the meat. But some weaker Christians could not see it that way, so they could not eat the meat without hurting their consciences. The stronger Christian, then, had a perfect right to eat the meat, but he should be careful not to use his freedom in such a way as to offend a weaker brother. The Kingdom is of far more importance than any meat. The Christian must always be governed by Christian, not pagan, standards. In a way, these chapters are entirely obsolete; we do not have the problem of meat offered to idols. But the principle back of these chapters is a vital one and should help us greatly as we try to decide about problems that are really non-moral for ourselves; we should remember that we are social beings, that we have influence, that we should not use our freedom in such a way as to wreck the lives of others, that at times we should make sacrifices for the sake of the Kingdom.

V. *Christian worship, 11 - 14.* Christian women should be very careful to wear their veils and keep quiet in church. Christianity thinks most highly of women and has done much to really free women. But we must remember that Paul was talking here primarily to the women of Corinth in the first century. They must be very careful to preserve all the decencies of the time; the freedom of the Christian women must not make outsiders confuse Christianity with the pagan Aphrodite cult. Again we must separate between principles and temporary applications of those principles. Abuses had arisen in the celebration of the sacrament of the Lord's Supper. They had developed a Love Feast before the Sacrament; hard feelings had arisen between the rich and the poor; some were so full of food and wine that they were in no condition to celebrate the Sacrament. These abuses should be corrected. Then there were some who were abusing the Spiritual Gifts, especially the speaking with tongues. This phenomenon is not to be confused with the other tongues of Pentecost. Here they were speaking in unknown tongues; many were speaking at the same time; the Church services were becoming mad houses; emotionalism was running riot; again, Christianity was in danger of being confused with the more ecstatic pagan cults. Paul admits a certain value in emotionalism, even in tongues, it seems. But he gave them some directions: let not more than two or three speak in tongues at any service; let them speak one at a time; let them speak in Church only if there is an interpreter. We cannot help wondering if these directions did not serve to eliminate speaking with tongues in the church services. In the midst of this strange section on Spiritual gifts comes one of the gems of all literature, the hymn to the greatest of all the Spiritual gifts, love.

VI. *The resurrection of the dead, 15.* No funeral service is complete without some verses from this well-known chapter. There is life beyond death. The resurrection of Jesus is proved; it in turn proves immortality. The Christian may suffer and die here, but he may look forward to a glorious eternity with God.

VII. *Conclusion, 16.* Directions are given for the taking of the collection for the saints in Jerusalem. Paul tells of his plans for the future. Salutations.

An Outline of Second Corinthians

I. *Reconciliation, 1 - 7.* God has been good and has solved the troublesome problem that had brought the crisis. Paul defends himself and his actions during the period of crisis. He tells them how they should act toward the offender and, in general, how Christians should act in such periods of stress.

II. *The collection, 8 - 9.* Paul urges liberality in the collection to be sent to the poor Christians in Judaea. Follow the good example of the Macedonian Christians. God loves a cheerful giver.

III. *Concluding warnings, 10 - 13.* The crisis has passed, but they should be careful that it does not happen again. He hopes that it will not be necessary for him to come to them again in sorrow. Paul has the authority of an apostle, but he does not like to have to use it on such painful occasions. Farewell.

Romans

The city of Rome, the capital of the Roman Empire, was the most important city in the world in the first century. Paul realized its importance as a Christian center. A church was started in Rome before Paul could get there himself. Paul wanted to go to Rome, but he had been prevented. When he reaches Corinth on his third missionary journey, he is not very far from Rome. But even so, he has been taking up the collection for the Judaean Christians, and he must now go on to Jerusalem to take it to them. He hopes that the collection will be the means of helping those Christian Jews in their need and also of restoring him and his Gentile converts to their good graces. He realized that he was going on a dangerous mission, however, as the Jews had come to think of him as a renegade who was seeking to destroy Judaism. He was warned against going, time and again, but he felt that he must perform his duty. He and others feared that his life would be in danger, and succeeding events proved that their fears had not been groundless. Paul wants, some day, to get to Rome, but now he is afraid that he may never have that privilege. But if he cannot get there in person, he can at least send them a letter and tell them what he considers the most important truths of the Christian faith. He wants the Church in that influential city to be well grounded on the fundamentals of the faith. So he writes this letter from Corinth to Rome and goes on to Jerusalem. He does finally reach Rome himself, but as a prisoner, and only after several years of danger and imprisonment. Because of the conditions under which Romans was written, it has proved one of the most valuable books in the New Testament; it gives us what the greatest mind of the early Church considered the heart of the Christian system of thought.

The destination and place and time of writing are made very clear in the Epistle itself, especially when we compare it with the account of the latter part of the third missionary journey in Acts, from the twentieth chapter on. He tells of his wish to go to Rome, but his duty to go to Jerusalem, in Rom. 1:1-15 and 15:14-33. In the sixteenth chapter, he commends Phoebe of Cenchreae, the port of Corinth; he sends greetings from Timothy and Sopater, who were Paul's companions when he left Corinth, according to Acts 20:4; from Gaius, whom Paul had baptized in Corinth, according to I Cor. 1:14; and from Erastus, who remained in Corinth, according to II Tim. 4:20. These notices will not fit Paul's visit to Corinth on the second missionary journey, but they fit exactly the third. Even if the sixteenth chapter be not considered a part of the Epistle, which will be discussed later, the Epistle must be dated at Corinth or between there and Jerusalem; but if the sixteenth chapter is a part of the Epistle, it must be dated at Corinth itself, on the third missionary journey, about 56 A.D.

The Integrity of Romans

Some scholars think that chapter sixteen does not belong with the first fifteen chapters but is to be considered a letter of commendation for Phoebe, written from Corinth to Ephesus rather than to Rome.

Chapter 16 contains an unusually large number of salutations. How did Paul know so many people in Rome when he had never been there? He had been in Ephesus several years. This objection is not very strong when we remember how much traveling there was in the first century. Rome was a commercial center, and many of Paul's former friends may have been in Rome at the time. And it is only natural that Paul should have made the most of those friends in writing to a Church which he had never visited.

Among the salutations was one to Priscilla and Aquila. In Acts 18:18-26, we see that they had gone from Corinth to Ephesus with Paul on his second missionary journey. When Paul wrote I Corinthians from Ephesus on the third journey, they are still in Ephesus and send their salutation along with the church that is in their house (I Cor. 16:19). In Rom. 16:3-5, Paul sends greetings to them and the church that is in their house. Some say that it is highly improbable that in the year or so between the writing of I Corinthians and Romans they would have left Ephesus and gone to Rome and established a Church in their house there. Possibly improbable, but by no means impossible. Travel was easy. They were travelers; Acts 18:1-3 tells that they had come from Italy because the Emperor Claudius had ordered the Jews to leave Rome; they came to Corinth, and then on to Ephesus. Is it unreasonable to think that they went back to Rome after Claudius' attempt to get rid of the Jews proved a failure? And is it unreasonable to think that they soon had a church in their house in Rome, a kind of cottage prayer meeting?

Rom. 16:5 also contains a salutation for Epaenetus, "who is the first-fruits of Asia unto Christ." Ephesus was in the Roman province of Asia. Epaenetus could have stayed in Ephesus or have gone on to Rome; in either case he could have been appropriately called "the first-fruits of Asia."

There is a benediction at the end of chapter 15.[3] It looks as if Paul is closing his Epistle there. But that does not prove that chapter 16 could not have been part of the same letter, possibly as a postscript. To end a letter after every benediction would prove too much if it proved anything, because there are benedictions at 15:33 and 16:20 and 16:25-27, and some manuscripts have even another one at 16:24. No one urges the splitting of the sixteenth chapter into several parts after each benediction.

It must be admitted that these objections to the integrity of the Epistle, and other minor ones that have been raised, carry some weight when taken together, though no one can be considered conclusive. It is possible that chapter 16 went to Ephesus. But if so, why did it become attached to a letter that went to Rome? What became of its salutation? Why does no manuscript exist giving these as two letters? There is some doubt, of course, but most Conservatives and many others believe that the balance of probability is in favor of the integrity of the Epistle. The first fifteen chapters were certainly written by Paul to Rome, probably from Corinth; the sixteenth chapter was certainly written by Paul from Corinth, probably to Rome; there is a high degree of probability that all sixteen chapters were written by Paul to Rome from Corinth.

---

[3] The newly discovered P^{46} even puts the long benediction, 16:25-27, at the end of chap. 15.

An Outline of the Contents

I. *Introduction, 1:1-17.* Paul salutes the Church, tells his interest in them, and states the theme of the Epistle, salvation by faith in Jesus Christ.

II. *Salvation needed, 1:18 - 3:20.* All men have enough knowledge of God to be responsible. Yet no man has lived up to the light that he has. Men rebelled against God, so God let men go. The picture of men's degradation is terrible, but it is true to the facts. Jews, as well as Gentiles, are under the just condemnation of a holy God. Deliverance is surely needed.

III. *Salvation provided, 3:21 - 5:21.* God has provided a way of deliverance from sin through Jesus Christ. This salvation is offered freely to all who have faith in Him. Justification is by faith, not by law. Paul shows that this way of salvation is the one taught even in the Old Testament, and also that it is a way that works in human experience. As sin came into the world by one man, so deliverance from sin has come by the one Son of Man.

IV. *Objections refuted, 6-7.* The doctrine of salvation by faith may be misunderstood, Paul realizes. He anticipates some objections that may be raised. No matter what form the objection takes, the conclusion is the same: the doctrine allows the believer to continue in sin. Paul vigorously denies this. One who has true faith in Christ has entered into a vital union with Him Who knows no sin; he has been released from the obligation of the law, but he has taken upon himself the obligation to a holy God. This doctrine does not prove that the law is a bad thing, but only that it is not able in itself to save a man; it shows man his need of salvation.

V. *Some benefits of salvation, 8.* The believer in

Christ is not condemned before God. He is no longer under the law but under the Spirit. He is an heir of God, a joint-heir with Jesus Christ. He is to inherit the eternal glories by and by. Even now God is making all things work together for good for him. God is for us, no matter who may be against us.

VI. *The Problem of the Jews, 9 - 11.* Salvation has been provided by the Christ who came in fulfilment of the Jewish prophecies, but the majority of the Jews are rejecting the Gospel. The Gentiles have the right to ask: "How do you expect us to accept Him when His own people have rejected Him?" This was a grave problem for the missionary to the Gentiles and one that gave him much sorrow, because he loved his kinsmen. Paul calls attention to the fact that the blessings promised by God had not been received by all the natural descendants of Abraham, but only by those who had the faith that Abraham had, his spiritual children. God has the right to choose whom He will, in any nation. The Jews of Paul's day were just following in the footsteps of many of their rebellious fathers. God is using the rejection of the Jews to send the gospel into the Gentile world. In God's own time and way all of the elect, Jews and Gentiles, will be gathered into the kingdom. We cannot always understand the workings of God's providence, but we can always trust Him to work everything for the good of those that love Him.

VII. *The Christian life, 12:1 - 15:12.* Jesus died as a sacrifice for our sins; we should present our bodies at least as living sacrifices for Him. True Christian faith is a living thing that turns a sinner into a saint. Various individual and social obligations are presented in a forceful, striking way.

VIII. *Conclusion, 15:13 - 16:27.* Paul salutes a long list of his friends who are now in Rome. He tells of his plans for the future, which he hopes will allow him to come to them. He weaves several benedictions into these concluding verses.

The Prison Epistles

After Paul wrote his letter to the Romans from Corinth, he went on to Jerusalem with the collections, as he had planned. But he did run into the anticipated difficulties there and had to be rescued by the Roman army and taken to Caesarea for safe keeping. After two years in prison there, he despaired of a fair trial and appealed to Caesar. After the long journey and shipwreck, he reached Rome as a prisoner. He was allowed to stay under guard in his own hired house; the Book of Acts closes when he had been there for two years.

Four of Paul's letters are commonly called the prison epistles, Ephesians, Colossians, Philemon, and Philippians. II Timothy was also written from an imprisonment, but it is best considered with the pastoral epistles. Col. 4:3 and 4:18 mention Paul's bonds. In Philemon 9, Paul calls himself a prisoner of Jesus Christ, and in 13 he mentions his bonds. Ephesians 3:1 and 4:1 speak of Paul as a prisoner, and in 6:20 Paul calls himself an ambassador in bonds. In Philippians Paul speaks of his bonds in 1: 7, 13, and 16.

It had long been taken for granted that these letters were written during the Roman imprisonment of Acts 28:16-31, but in recent years attempts have been made to assign them to the Caesarean imprisonment of Acts 23:33 - 26:32, or to a supposed imprisonment at Ephesus during his stay there, Acts 19:1-41.

The case for the Caesarean imprisonment is very weak. Paul was in prison there, but we cannot well fit any of the prison epistles into the conditions there. Philip of Caesarea is not mentioned in any of the salutations. Paul's expectations of release were more natural from Rome than from Caesarea. The runaway slave would have been much more likely to have gone to Rome than Caesarea. The intercourse with Philippi is more easily explained from Rome, also the mention of the praetorian guard in Philippians 1:13 and those of Caesar's household in Philippians 4:22.

There are certain interesting arguments in favor of Ephesus. Ephesus is much closer to Colosse and Philippi than Rome is. Even Ephesians may have been a circular letter written from Ephesus to the churches in the vicinity. The runaway slave could easily have gone from Colosse to the great metropolis of Ephesus. The intercourse with the Philippians could more easily have taken place with Paul in Ephesus than in Rome. A praetorian guard is known to have been in Ephesus, so that that mention would fit Ephesus as well as Rome. Even "they of Caesar's household" may have applied to the Roman officials in Ephesus. His expectation of paying a visit to the Philippians would fit well with Ephesus, because we know that he went from there to Philippi. Practically all of Paul's companions mentioned in the salutations are known to have been with him in Ephesus. But the Book of Acts does not mention any imprisonment at Ephesus. Of course, Acts does not tell everything that happened to Paul, but we would expect rather strongly the mention of anything as important as an imprisonment. The arguments for Ephesus are by no means conclusive; Ephesus must be considered a possibility but not a probability.

We know that Paul was in prison in Rome. The praetorian guard and Caesar's household are most natural in Rome. He had the freedom of his own house for the composition of letters. The runaway slave may easily have gone to Rome to try to lose himself in the crowds at the capital. Contact was easy enough with Philippi and Ephesus and Colosse. Many friends who were with Paul in Ephesus may have been with him from time to time in Rome. The traditional assignment of all the prison epistles to the Roman imprisonment remains rather highly probable, though we cannot consider it quite certain.

The Authorship of the Prison Epistles

All of these epistles name Paul as their author and give many personal notes that fit well the Acts account of the life of Paul. There have been some scholars who have called in question the Pauline authorship of some or all of this group of letters. The case against the Pauline authorship of Colossians, Philemon, and Philippians is extremely weak, and practically all scholars believe that Paul wrote them. The type of Gnostic heresy against which Paul is arguing need not be dated in the second century as some have claimed. The Church at Philippi may well have had bishops and deacons during Paul's life, as Philippians 1:1 says. The thought and style of the letters cause no real difficulty when we compare them with other Paulines.

The case against the Pauline authorship of Ephesians is somewhat stronger. The style seems somewhat different; the author uses many words that are not found in other Pauline letters. Paul spent three years at Ephesus on his third missionary journey, yet Ephesians is a very impersonal letter; he does not send salutations to a single individual. Some have thought that Ephesians was written by some unknown admirer of Paul, who wove together certain Pauline thoughts and phrases taken largely from Colossians. No one of these arguments is quite conclusive, however. Some differences in style and vocabulary are entirely natural; Paul was an educated person, not bound by a limited vocabulary or a single style. The impersonal tone is a fact, but it does not disprove the Pauline authorship.

Paul says in Eph. 6:21 that Tychicus was to tell them about him; he may also well have carried Paul's salutations. Then there is evidence that Ephesians was a circular letter, and personal salutations to members of just one church would have been out of place in such a letter. The evidence for the Pauline authorship is probably much stronger than that against it.

The Dates of the Prison Epistles

We may date the two years that Paul was in Rome in his own hired house roughly as about 59 to 61 A.D. These four letters, then were probably written sometime between those dates. But we can be a little more definite than that. Three of the letters, Ephesians, Colossians, and Philemon, were almost surely written at the same time and carried to their destinations by the same person. Tychicus is mentioned as the bearer in Eph. 6:21 and Col. 4:7. Col. 4:9 says that Onesimus, the runaway slave, was one of the Colossians and that he was with Tychicus; Tychicus almost certainly brought the little letter and the runaway slave from Paul to Philemon in Colosse. These three letters were probably written together towards the beginning of the imprisonment. There is nothing to require a long time in prison in any of them, and none of them mentions his expectation of release which we find in Philippians. We may date these first three prison epistles rather certainly as together in 59 or 60.

Philippians must be considered separately. It did not go to Asia Minor but to Macedonia. It is probably to be dated towards the close of the imprisonment, about 61, for several reasons. Phil. 1:12 ff suggests that he had been in Rome for some time; 1: 25 and 2: 23, 24 tell that he was expecting to be released so that he could visit them; 2:25-30 and 4:10 tell us of events that must have taken some time: the Philippians had heard that Paul was in prison and had sent him a gift by Epaphroditus; Epaphroditus had become seriously ill; the Philippians had heard of the sickness and had become worried; Epaphroditus had learned of their sorrow over his illness; Epaphroditus had recovered and was going home, probably carrying the letter with him.

The Destination of Ephesians

An interesting problem is raised by the fact that the words "in Ephesus" in Eph. 1: 1 are omitted by some of the very best textual authorities; namely, the two earliest and best Greek uncial manuscripts, Aleph and B, the very earliest papyrus P^{46}; the Greek cursive, 1739; Origen, Marcion; and Tertullian said that other heretics like Marcion omitted the words. The evidence for the omission is very strong. Without the words, the Greek is somewhat rough, but it is possible. Marcion and some of the heretics called the letter Laodiceans.

These facts, and the fact that the letter has so few personal touches though Paul knew Ephesus so well, call for some explanation. Probably the letter was a circular letter, intended to be sent to the various churches in Asia Minor. In Col. 4:16, Paul tells the Colossians to read the letter from Laodicea. This circular letter may have been for Ephesus, Laodicea, Colosse, and possibly others. One copy without any named destination may have been circulated, or various copies with or without the various destinations named. Marcion and others seem to have known the connection with Laodicea. The later manuscripts give the connection with the more famous Ephesus, while the earliest manuscripts leave out the destination in 1:1, though even they connect the epistle with Ephesus in the title to the epistle.

The Epistle, then, probably went to Ephesus and other nearby cities. Paul had spent three years in Ephesus on his third missionary journey, and he may have had some contact with the other churches at the same time.

The mention by Marcion and Col. 4:16 of a letter to the Laodiceans excited the curiosity of some of the early Christians who did not identify that letter with Ephesians. Sometime between the second and fourth centuries, someone produced a letter purporting to have been Paul's letter to the Laodiceans. This letter is clearly a forgery, a very crude mixture of phrases taken from Paul's letters. For a time it had a measure of popularity, but it was quite correctly excluded from the New Testament canon.

The Contents of Ephesians

The division between the doctrinal and practical sections is clearly marked, but subdivisions are not so easy to see.

I. *Doctrinal, 1 - 3.* Christians are chosen by God in Christ. This choice is the working out of God's eternal purpose. They were chosen from being sons of wrath to being sons of God. This is the gospel that Paul preaches and urges the Church to make known.

II. *Practical, 4-6.* The obligations and privileges of the sons of God. A life of service in the Church. A life of witness to the world. A life of love in the family. A life of strength. A life of prayer.

Colossians

Colosse was a city near Laodicea, not so very far from Ephesus. So far as we know, Paul had never been in Colosse himself, though he was for three years in Ephesus. One of the earnest Colossian Christians, Epaphras, met Paul in Rome and told him some things about them that called forth this letter.[4] The Colossians were striving earnestly to be Christians, but they were

---

[4] Col. 1:7, 8; 4:12, 13.

in danger of certain false doctrines. The error seems to have been much like that mentioned in II Peter, Jude, and the letters in Revelation, and hinted at in the Pastoral Epistles. It was probably an early form of the Gnosticism which became so prominent in the second century. Paul commends them for their good points, but he warns them very definitely against the errors of false doctrine.

I. *Introduction and thanksgiving, 1: 1-8.*

II. *Doctrinal, 1:9 - 3:4.* Hold fast to the true doctrine and avoid error. Heresy can be persuasive. Most heresy is an attempt to substitute human philosophy and ritualism for a divine revelation. Most heresy centers about the person and work of Christ. Combat heresy by presenting the true view of Christ, the God-man, the divine Savior, the living Lord.

III. *Practical, 3:5 - 4:6.* Avoid heresy in life as well as in doctrine. Live in all relationships lives governed by faith, hope, and love.

IV. *Concluding salutations, 4: 7-18.*

PHILEMON

Col. 4:9 tells us that Onesimus was a Colossian. From that and the little epistle to Philemon, we can reconstruct the background fairly accurately. Philemon was a wealthy member of the church at Colosse, and Onesimus was one of his slaves. Verse 19 indicates that Philemon had probably been converted under Paul's ministry, we do not know where, possibly in Ephesus. The slave, Onesimus, runs away from his master and seeks to lose himself in the crowds of Rome. But in Rome he came under the influence of Paul and was converted to Christ. His duty then was to make restitution for his past sins; he must go back to his master. Paul writes this charming little personal note to go along with the returned slave to Philemon. He urges Philemon to forgive Onesimus for his past sins, suggesting that he charge them to his account; Philemon owes Paul more than Onesimus owed to Philemon. He urges Philemon to receive Onesimus back kindly — "as a servant, but above a servant, a brother beloved." Paul hopes to visit Philemon himself when he is released from prison.

This little letter is purely a personal one, but it gives us a beautiful insight into the charm and courtesy of the man Paul and into the high sense of duty that he believed in and taught. Paul might have kept Onesimus for his personal servant, but for the sake of Onesimus and Philemon, Onesimus should go back.

Philemon has been used to justify human slavery. But Paul simply recognized the existence of the institution and thought that there was nothing that he could do at the time to do away with it. We are all glad that civilization, in accordance with Christian principles, has abolished slavery.

Philippians

Philippi was a great city in Macedonia, a Roman colony. It was the first city on the continent of Europe where Paul preached after he saw the vision of the man of Macedonia. Acts 16:12-40 tells us of his stay there on his second missionary journey. A women's prayer meeting became a Christian church. Lydia took Paul into her home. The healing of the girl with a spirit of divination got Paul and Silas thrown into prison. Their miraculous release led to the conversion of the jailor and his household. Then they went on down to the southern part of Greece. Paul probably visited Philippi also on his third journey, though it is not mentioned by name. The Philippians were very solicitous for Paul's welfare. From time to time they sent money and provisions to him. When they heard that he was in a Roman prison, they sent one of their number, Epaphroditus, with provisions, to minister to his needs. Epaphroditus stayed in Rome to serve Paul. While he was there, he became seriously ill, and his friends in Philippi heard of it and became concerned. Epaphroditus was grieved that he had caused them grief. But he has recovered now, and Paul sends him back to Philippi along with a letter of commendation and thanks.[5]

Many think that the Church at Philippi was Paul's favorite church; there were certainly close ties between them. Philippians is a very intimate, personal letter. Although it was written from a Roman imprisonment, its main thought seems to have been joy; the words "joy" and "rejoice" are used sixteen times in the four short chapters.[6]

I. *Introduction, 1:1-11.* Greetings. Thanksgiving for their faith and lives. Prayer for continued growth.

II. *God's care of Paul, 1:12-30.* God had overruled adversity. Though a prisoner, Paul was a preacher. The guards that kept Paul were being converted. Paul is satisfied to live or to die—"to live is Christ; to die is gain."

III. *Paul's appeal for spiritual unity, 2.* Have brotherly love. Be ruled by the spirit of Christ, humility and sacrifice. Strive earnestly for contentment, peace, and purity. Timothy will be sent to help them; meanwhile, Epaphroditus is being sent back.

IV. *The danger of false doctrine, 3.* Beware of those who teach ceremonialism as a substitute for the true gospel. Paul gives his own experience with law and faith; he urges them to imitate him.

V. *Conclusion, 4.* The women of the church should

---

5 Philip. 2:25 ff; 4:10 ff.

6 16 times in the better text followed by the Revised Version; 17, in the King James Version.

live at peace with one another. All should live lives of joy, beauty, and strength. Paul thanks them again for their kindness. Salutations and benediction.

The Pastoral Epistles

First and Second Timothy and Titus are called the pastoral epistles, because they were written to two young preachers by the old preacher, Paul. They deal primarily with matters of Church organization and discipline.

Authorship

The Epistles name the Apostle Paul as their author, and all the tradition that we have on the subject gives them to Paul. Many personal references in the Epistles fit the life of Paul as we know it. Many modern scholars do not believe that Paul wrote them, however. Let us consider some of the reasons given against the Pauline authorship.

The vocabulary contains a large number of words that are not found in the other Pauline epistles. A glance at the appendix in Thayer's Lexicon or the introduction of any critical commentary will suffice to prove the fact. But does the fact necessitate the belief that Paul did not write the pastorals? Not quite. The subject-matter in these letters is different from that of the others; different words were called for. Paul, an educated man, had a large vocabulary at his disposal. Paul used scribes from time to time, and different scribes may have had something to do with different vocabularies.

There are notes about Paul's journeys throughout the pastoral epistles that will not fit into the Book of Acts. To believe that Paul wrote the pastorals and did the things mentioned in them, it is necessary to think that Paul was released from his imprisonment in Rome, that he made further journeys not told in Acts, and that he was put into prison again in Rome. It is true that Acts does not tell us about any of this, but it is just as true that Acts does not say that Paul died after he had been in prison in his own hired house for two years. These later journeys may not have been mentioned in Acts because Acts may have been written at the time when Paul had been in prison for two years, or they were to have been recorded in a later volume which may have been written and lost or which may have been anticipated and never written. There is some evidence that Paul may have been automatically released from his first imprisonment because two years had passed and his accusers had failed to prove their case against him. The Muratorian Canon and possibly Clement of Rome bear testimony to other journeys of Paul, though they may have been influenced by the notes in the pastorals or Paul's statement in Romans that he wished to visit Spain.

Some feel that the ecclesiastical development of the churches proves a date later than the life of Paul. Elders, bishops, and deacons are mentioned. But the words "bishop" and "elder" were used interchangeably in the pastorals; elders came from Old Testament times and may easily have been adopted early by the Christian Church. Acts 6 tells of the origin of the deacons; deacons were in use before the death of Paul if we can accept the truthfulness of Acts 6 or an early dating for Acts. We must be careful not to date the pastorals too late, because early in the second century we get the rise of a different kind of bishop, that similar to the Episcopal bishop today; and we have no intimation of anything like that in the pastorals.

Some feel that creedal development had gone further in the pastorals than it could have gone in Paul's day. "The faith" is a very definite thing, quite distinct from the beliefs of the heretics. Scripture is spoken of as the inspired Word of God. Conservatives have no difficulties with these facts, and others admit that they are by no means conclusive; only those who take a very slow view of the evolution of the doctrine of the Church feel much force in this argument.

Marcion does not include the pastorals in his canon. But Marcion was a heretic and probably did not like what Paul had to say about heresy in the pastorals. If we followed Marcion's canon, we should have to omit quite a few other books, too, including all of our gospels except Luke.

Some feel that the traces of Gnosticism cannot be accounted for in Paul's lifetime. But Colossians was almost certainly by Paul, and it seems to have the same heresy. An early dating of II Peter and Jude would also put Gnosticism in Paul's day.

Many who believe that Paul did not write the pastorals as they stand today at least believe that there are genuine Pauline parts in them. Practically all Conservatives and many others, however, believe that Paul wrote them in their entirety.

Dates and Places

If Paul did not write the pastorals, we know really nothing about their dates or places of origin; the different scholars fit them as best they can into their own ideas of the evolution of the Christian Church.

If Paul did write them, we still have problems, but we can know a little more. Paul was released from his first Roman imprisonment about 61 A.D. He was almost certainly martyred by Nero by 67 A.D., possibly 64 in connection with the burning of Rome. The pastorals were written sometime between his release and his martyrdom. Paul had made some journeys after his release, but we do not know how long to allow for them. II Timothy seems definitely to have been written shortly before Paul's martyrdom; he speaks of himself as a prisoner in 1: 8, 16 and 2: 9; he is looking for death in 4: 6; the last verses of the Epistle tell us that most of his friends had deserted him. II Timothy was the last of all the Pauline letters, written before his martyrdom, before 67 A.D. I Timothy and Titus were written sometime before that but after 61. Any datings closer than these must be guesses.

Paul wrote the letters to Timothy to Ephesus, where Paul had left him as the young preacher. Titus had likewise been left on the island of Crete, and he received his letter there.

Paul wrote II Timothy from his second Roman imprisonment, but we do not know where he was when he wrote I Timothy and Titus. I Timothy 1: 3 says that Paul went to Macedonia after he left Timothy at Ephesus; he may have written I Timothy and Titus from some place in Macedonia, but we cannot be in the least sure.

Outlines of the Contents

I Timothy

I. *Instructions concerning the Church, 1-3.* Warning against false teachers. Instructions concerning worship. The character of church officers. Christ, the center of true Christian faith.

II. *Instructions concerning the Minister, 4-6.* Timothy must avoid all false teaching. He must know how to deal with the different classes of persons in the Church. Be a man of God; fight the good fight; lay hold on eternal life.

Titus

I. *Salutation, 1: 1-4.*
II. *Church officers, 1:5-16.*

III. *Duties of various classes of members, 2.* All should be zealous of good works.

IV. *The Christian as a member of society, 3: 1-8.*

V. *The Christian and heresy, 3: 9-11.*

VI. *Conclusion, 3: 12-15.*

II Timothy

I. *Introduction, 1.* Salutation and personal notes. Paul's Christian confidence in spite of trials.

II. *Timothy's duties, 2:1 - 4:5.* He must be strong, must be true in doctrine, must grow in spiritual matters. He must train others, like himself, to carry on the truth, even in the face of an increasing heresy.

III. *Paul's faith and hope, 4: 6-8.*

IV. *Conclusion, 4:9-22.* Personal directions. Salutations. Benediction.

X

THE EPISTLE TO THE HEBREWS

Authorship

The King James Version has the title, "The Epistle of Paul the Apostle to the Hebrews," which came from the late Syrian type of manuscripts. The American Revised Version, following the earliest and best manuscripts, has simply, "The Epistle to the Hebrews."

The Epistle does not name its author. All of the thirteen Pauline epistles that we have studied begin, "Paul, an apostle . . ." Hebrews has no salutation whatever.

From the earliest times there has been doubt as to the authorship of Hebrews. The Epistle was in use at least as early as the letter of Clement of Rome to the Corinthians,[1] about 95 A.D., though it was not included in Marcion's canon or the Muratorian canon.

The earliest evidence as to the authorship comes from Clement of Alexandria, about 200 A.D. Eusebius, in *Church History* vi, 14, quotes him as saying, "that the Epistle is Paul's, and that it was written to Hebrews in the Hebrew language, and that Luke translated it with zealous care and published it to the Greeks; whence it is that the same complexion of style is found in the translation of this Epistle and in the Acts; that the

[1] For parallels, see Westcott, **The Epistle to the Hebrews,** lxiii f.

phrase 'Paul an Apostle' was not placed at the head of the Epistle for good reason; for, he says, in writing to Hebrews who had formed a prejudice against him and viewed him with suspicion, he was wise not to repel them at the beginning by setting his name there." Clement recognizes difficulties with the Pauline authorship; at most, he can say that he believes that Paul wrote a Hebrew (or Aramaic) original that was translated by Luke. His theory may possibly be true, but the Greek of the Epistle does not look like a translation; it is entirely too smooth and idiomatic.

Origen, about 245, said[2]: "Every one who understands how to judge language would acknowledge that the character of the writing of the Epistle to the Hebrews does not have the idiom of the Apostle, who acknowledged that he was unlearned in speech, that is, in expression; but the Epistle is more Greek in the composition of the speech. But, on the other hand, anyone who attends to the apostolic reading would agree that the thoughts of the Epistle are marvelous and in no way inferior to the apostolic writings. . . . If I were to express my own opinion I should say that the thoughts are the thoughts of the apostle, but the language and composition that of one who recalled from memory, and, as it were, made notes of what was said by his master. If, therefore, any church holds this Epistle to be Paul's, let it be approved for this also (as for holding unquestioned truths), for it was not without reason that the men of old time have handed it down as Paul's. But who wrote the Epistle God only knows certainly. The account that has reached us is twofold: some say Clement, who became bishop of the Romans, wrote the Epistle; others, that Luke wrote it, who wrote the Gospel and the Acts. But on this I will say no more." Origen,

[2] Quoted in Eusebius, **Church History**, vi, 25.

too, recognized difficulties with the Pauline authorship. At most, he could claim that the thoughts were Paul's. Clement of Rome and Luke are suggested as responsible for the Greek that we have, whether as translator or scribe he does not say. He admits that God alone knows who wrote the Epistle.

Clement and Origen think of the Epistle as having Pauline authority back of it, and that is the important thing for them, rather than who was responsible for the Greek text as we have it. Yet the later Alexandrians, Dionysius, Theognostus, and Peter, following their lead, went on and attributed the Epistle to Paul without question. Eusebius believed that Paul wrote it in Hebrew and Clement of Rome translated it, though he notices that some people still rejected it.[3]

Although Alexandria and the East came generally to receive the Epistle as Pauline in the third century, Rome and the West did not. Hippolytus (Rome, about 200-240) and Irenaeus (Lyons, about 185) were acquainted with the Epistle but held that it was not Paul's, if we may believe the testimony of the sixth century Stephen Gobar.[4] The Epistle is not quoted by Novatian, Arnobius, or Lactantius; Westcott concludes that they did not recognize its canonical authority.

Toward the end of the fourth century, Jerome and Augustine begin to swing the West to the Pauline view. Jerome is himself doubtful about the matter, as we see from his formulae of quoting the Epistle: "The Epistle which, under the name of Paul, is written to the Hebrews"; "He who writes to the Hebrews"; "The Apostle Paul, or whoever else wrote the Epistle to the Hebrews"; "The Apostle Paul in the Epistle to the Hebrews, which the Latin custom does not receive." He mentions that the Greek writers accept it as Paul's, although

[3] **Church History,** iii, 3; iii, 38.

[4] Cf. Westcott, **op. cit.,** pp. lxiv f.

many ascribe it either to Barnabas or Clement.[5] Jerome included the Epistle in his canon, thinking that it was wiser to include than to exclude a good book, and moved by authority of the Eastern Church. Augustine sometimes reckons it among Paul's letters, and sometimes he cites it anonymously. Sometimes he calls attention to the doubts entertained about it by others. But he professes to accept it himself because of the authority of the Eastern Churches. In the Council of Hippo in 393, and in the first Council of Carthage in 398, the canonical list runs: "of the Apostle Paul, thirteen epistles; of the same to the Hebrews, one." But in the second Council of Carthage in 419, even this meaningless distinction is lost, and the list runs: "of the epistles of Paul in number, fourteen." And from the fifth century to the Reformation, the Epistle was generally accepted as Paul's without question.

Let us look at the Epistle itself.

We have seen that the title in the earliest manuscripts says nothing about Paul, and that the Epistle itself does not name its author.

The author seems to have been personally acquainted with those to whom he wrote, judging from 6:9 f; 10:34; 13:7, 19. In 13:23 he speaks of Timothy as a mutual friend.

The author seems to put himself in the second generation of believers in 2:3 f: "How shall we escape if we neglect so great salvation; which at the first began to be spoken by the Lord, and was confirmed unto us by them that heard him; God also bearing witness, both with signs and wonders, and with divers miracles, and gifts of the Holy Ghost, according to his own will?" This seems quite different from the

[5] Letter to Dardanus.

attitude taken by Paul in Gal. 1:1: "Paul, an apostle (not of men, neither by man, but by Jesus Christ, and God the Father, who raised him from the dead)," and Gal. 1:11, 12: "For I certify you, brethren, that the gospel which was preached of me is not after man. For I neither received it of man, neither was I taught it, but by the revelation of Jesus Christ."

The argument from style is always a precarious one, but here the case is quite marked. From the earliest times, it has been noted that the style of the Epistle is quite unlike the style of the other Pauline letters. The Greek is highly polished; it is closer to the literary Classical Greek than that found in any other New Testament book, with the possible exception of Luke-Acts. Paul frequently digresses; he starts a sentence and never finishes it; he changes from one construction to another. But in Hebrews there is always perfect smoothness and balance; each sentence and paragraph fits exactly into place; there is never anything ungrammatical.

Let us look briefly at some other possible authors that have been suggested.

Clement of Alexandria suggested that Paul wrote the Epistle in Hebrew and that Luke translated it into Greek. It is true that the style of Hebrews is quite like that of Luke-Acts, but the likeness is not definite enough to prove identity of authorship. Clement's theory carries with it a belief in a Hebrew original, which is most unlikely, and which casts doubt on the whole theory. This theory has had the support of some modern scholars, but it can be considered at best only an interesting possibility.

Tertullian and Jerome and some moderns think that the author was Barnabas. Barnabas suits very well; he was close enough to Paul to know his thoughts; he was a Levite, interested in matters of ritual; he was a native of Cyprus, where good Greek was used; he was influential in the church at Jerusalem. But if he wrote it, why did his name get lost and Paul's become associated with it? Barnabas can be considered only another interesting possibility.

Eusebius and Jerome bear witness to the theory that Paul wrote the letter in Hebrew and that Clement of Rome translated it into Greek. Erasmus and a few modern scholars have followed this theory. There are certain superficial similarities between Hebrews and Clement's letter to the Corinthians, but there are even more important differences. And again, this theory suffers from its belief in a Hebrew original.

From the time of the Reformation on, many other guesses have been made. Luther suggested Apollos, and he has had some followers. Several modern scholars have supported Priscilla and Aquila. Others have suggested Silvanus, Peter, Aristion, and Philip the deacon. But none of these has any ancient testimony, and all of them must be considered only interesting guesses.

After considering all the evidence available, we have to come back to the statement made long ago by Origen: "As to who wrote the Epistle to the Hebrews God alone knows the truth." Our modern pride may resent the necessity of such a negative conclusion, but we may remember that we know very few of the authors of the Old Testament books. The Epistle is in thorough harmony with the teaching of Paul, and it may well be said to carry Pauline authority with it; its acceptance into the canon may be justified by that fact. But there seems to be more evidence against the Pauline authorship of the Greek Epistle than we have for it. One of the others suggested may have been the author or translator, but we shall probably never be able to find out until the time comes when we shall know all things fully.

Date

If Paul wrote the Epistle, it was written before his martyrdom, probably some time before 67 A.D.; there is nothing in the Epistle to justify a more definite date. If Paul did not write it, it was probably written sometime in the first century, as it seems rather clearly to have been used by Clement of Rome about 95 A.D. The mention of Timothy in 13:23 makes us believe that he was still alive, thereby suggesting a first century date. The note in 2:3, 4 suggesting that the author belonged to the second generation of Christians points, probably, to the latter half of the first century. Somewhere between about 50 and 95 is as close as we are justified in placing it. As nothing is said about the destruction of Jerusalem, it was probably written before 70 or quite a few years later; if it had been written shortly after 70, we cannot see how the author could have avoided mentioning such an important event, one with such a close bearing on his whole argument.

Place of Writing and Destination

The title in all the manuscripts says "to Hebrews," and the contents of the Epistle suggest most strongly that it was written to some special group of Hebrews. Only a few modern scholars doubt that, and their reasons for doubt are not convincing. But where were those Hebrews located, and where was the author when he wrote? We cannot tell. 13:24 says, "They of Italy salute you." That may mean that the author was in Italy, possibly Rome, when he wrote. It may mean, however, that he was writing to Italy, and he was sending the salutations of the Italians back to Italy from wherever he was at the time. Some of the later manuscripts say that the Epistle was written from Rome or Italy, but their evidence is late and probably came from an interpretation of the note in 13:24. The Epistle may have been written to Jerusalem, the center of Judaism; but there were Jews in practically every city in the Roman Empire. It was written to some group of Jews, probably to or from Rome.

The Occasion

Although we cannot know just when, where, to whom, and by whom the Epistle was written, the general background is rather clear. The persons addressed were Jews who had become Christians. As members of the Jewish religion they had the protection of the Roman government; Judaism was considered a permitted religion because it was an old, well-established one. Christians were not accorded that protection; at times Rome did not think Christianity important enough to notice the Christians; but at times Rome did take notice, and Rome could make it mighty hard. Usually the Jews were persecuting the Christians in various ways. In many ways it was far harder to be a Christian than to be a Jew. Some of the Jewish Christians, then, began to wonder if there was enough difference between Christianity and Judaism to justify all that their Christianity was costing them. The Epistle to the Hebrews was written to meet that situation. The author makes many comparisons between Christianity and Judaism, showing in each case the superiority of Christianity. He does not condemn Judaism, but he shows that true Judaism is fulfilled in Christianity. In showing the superiority of Christianity, the author shows also its finality; it is the ultimate, perfect religion, beyond which we cannot hope to go. Thus this remarkably beautiful Epistle has a vital meaning for our time as it had for the first century.

An Outline of the Contents

I. *The finality of Christianity, 1:1-4.*

II. *The superiority of the Christian mediator. 1:5 - 2:18.* Christ is better than the angels. The author proves this by Scripture and draws some lessons from this truth.

III. *The superiority of the Christian founder, 3 - 4.* Jesus is better than Moses and Joshua. Moses may be likened to a servant in a house; Jesus, to the master over the house. It was wrong to disobey the law of Moses; how much more, the principles of Christ? Joshua led the people into a temporary, imperfect rest; Jesus leads His people into the perfect rest of eternity. Let us strive to enter into that glorious rest.

IV. *The superiority of the Christian priesthood, 5:1 - 10:18.* Christ is a priest superior to the Aaronic priesthood. Jesus was called by God to the priesthood, as was Aaron. Jesus, the God-man, was able to be a perfect go-between between man and God. Jesus brings all the benefits of the Holy Spirit, which should not be neglected. Jesus was not of the lineage of Aaron, but was a priest after the order of Melchisedec, a superior order, to whom even Abraham paid reverence. The Aaronic priests offered frequent, imperfect, typical sacrifices for sin; Jesus offered the perfect, real sacrifice of Himself once for all. The sanctuary of the old priests was but a type of the real sanctuary into which the Great Highpriest, Jesus, entered. The covenant of the old dispensation was good, but the new covenant is far better. Again the perfect sacrifice of Christ is emphasized.

V. *Concluding exhortations, 10:19 - 13:25.* The author has been giving exhortations from time to time throughout the Epistle, but this section is given almost wholly to them. He urges his readers to appropriate for themselves all the benefits of the superior, final Christian religion. Hold fast to the faith even in the face of the greatest hardships. Please God rather than men. The heroes of olden times lived glorious lives of faith; Christians ought to do even better. Run the good race; fight the good fight. Let us serve God acceptably in all our relationships. Salutations and benedictions.

XI

THE CATHOLIC EPISTLES

SEVEN of the shorter epistles of the New Testament have long been traditionally known as the Catholic or General Epistles: James, I and II Peter, I, II and III John, and Jude. Several of these letters are not really catholic, or universal, and the Epistle to the Hebrews may well be included in the group; but we may use the traditional grouping in spite of its limitations. It is to be noted, however, that the Epistles of John are treated in connection with the Johannine Literature in our treatment.

THE EPISTLE OF JAMES

Authorship

James 1:1 reads: "James, a servant of God and of the Lord Jesus Christ, to the twelve tribes which are scattered abroad, greeting." The Epistle is not anonymous; it is either pseudonymous, or it was written by some person by the name of James. But James was a very familiar name, and the author only claims to be "James, a servant of God and of the Lord Jesus Christ," or, in other words, a Christian by the name of James. He does not say that he was an apostle or the brother of Jesus, though he does not say that he was not. The fact that he does not trouble to identify himself more fully gives us some ground for thinking that he was a well-known James, *the* James.

Tradition as to the authorship is not very full or very early, but all that we have points to James the brother of Jesus, the early head of the Jerusalem Church. Origen, who died in 253 A.D., is the first known writer to quote the Epistle as Scripture and assign it to James the brother of Jesus, which he does in his *Commentary on Romans*, 4:8. At least five times he quotes from the Epistle and says that it was written by the Apostle James, by which he almost certainly means the brother of Jesus. In his *Commentary on John*, 19:6, he says: ". . . as we read in the current (*pheromene*) Epistle of James." Some have felt that the word "current" indicated doubt on the part of Origen, but that is not at all evident. Nor does the statement in the *Commentary on John*, 20:10, show any doubt for himself or any group in the Church. Eusebius, about 325, reports that there is doubt in the church. He divides our twenty-seven books of the New Testament into two classes, those recognized by all and those disputed but well known and recognized by many; he has a third list of spurious books. In *Church History* 3, 25, he includes in his disputed list "the epistle circulated under the name of James." In 2, 23, he tells about the martyrdom of James the Just and says: "The first of the epistles styled Catholic is said to be his. But I must remark that it is held to be spurious. Certainly not many old writers have mentioned it, nor yet the Epistle of Jude, which is also one of the Epistles called Catholic. But nevertheless we know that these have been publicly used with the rest in most churches." Eusebius seems to have no doubt in his own mind, but he reports the doubt of the Syrian Church, which had a small canon for a long time. Jerome, in *Illustrious Men*, 2, says that James, who is called the brother of the Lord, wrote one of the Catholic Epistles, but he reports the fact that some assert that it was written by someone else under James's name. James was not in the Muratorian Canon, which probably came from Rome about 200 A.D., or in any of the Syrian versions until the Peshitto of the early fifth century. It was in the Clermont List from Egypt about 300, in the canonical lists of Cyril of Jerusalem in 348 and Athanasius in 367, and in the great fourth-century manuscripts, Aleph and B, and in the canonical lists of the councils.

Besides 1:1, the Epistle gives nothing of a definite nature concerning the author, but there are certain hints that may be noted. The Epistle makes great use of the teachings of Jesus, especially of the Sermon on the Mount; this might well have been expected of a brother of Jesus. Like Jesus, too, the author makes great use of parables and figurative language. Hegesippus records the tradition that James the brother of Jesus was called "The Just"; the Epistle is primarily ethical, which accords well with that tradition. Acts 15 gives a speech made by James the brother of Jesus and a letter written by him; Mayor[1] points out a number of striking similarities between the Epistle and the 230 words of James's speech and letter. All of this accords with the general tradition, but it lacks much of being positive proof. Some have felt that the Greek of the Epistle is too good to have been written by the son of a Galilean carpenter; but James could have developed a good Greek style during his lifetime, or he could have used an educated scribe, which was frequently done. Some have felt that the absence of much doctrine shows that it came from the second century, when the Church ceased to be interested in theology and became interested in ethics; others have felt just as strongly that the absence of theology proves that

[1] The Epistle of St. James, J. B. Mayor, Macmillan, 1913, p. iii.

it was pre-Pauline; the truth is that we know too little about early Church history to assert that there was ever any time when the Church was interested only in ethics or only in theology—the two are by no means exclusive interests. Some have felt that the Epistle made use of literature produced after the death of James, proving that James could not have written it. For a fuller discussion of this highly technical problem, see the critical commentaries; we may say that this point is far from proved. There is evidently a very close connection with I Peter, but it is just as easy to think that Peter may have used James as the reverse.

We must leave the question of authorship as one that is not capable of final solution with our present knowledge. The case for James the brother of Jesus is weakened somewhat by the scantiness and lateness of the external evidence and the slowness with which the Epistle took an undisputed place in the canon, but still the case is rather strong. If he did not write it, we have no idea who did.

Date

The question of date is bound rather closely to that of authorship. If the brother of Jesus wrote it, it must be dated before his death. Josephus[2] says that James was killed by the high priest Ananus after the death of Festus, before the arrival of Albinus, which would be 62 A.D. This passage in Josephus is suspected of being an interpolation, though on very scanty grounds. Hegesippus[3], about 180, gives a long description of the death of James, which, he said, took place just before Vespasian besieged the Jews, which would be about 66 or 69 A.D. These traditions are

[2] Antiquities, 20, 9.
[3] In Eusebius, Church History, 2, 23.

contradictory, but they both point to the same decade, the sixties. If James wrote the Epistle, it was probably written in the sixties or before.

How late may the Epistle be placed if James did not write it? The Epistle is so short that it is impossible to be very certain as to its use by the early Fathers. Clement of Rome may possibly have used it at the close of the first century. There are more parallels with the Shepherd of Hermas, about 130; Justin Martyr, about 150, and Irenaeus, about 185, show some parallels. Clement of Alexandria, about 200, probably included James in his *Outlines*. Origen, about 250, definitely quotes the Epistle as James's. Nothing before 250 can be definitely proved to be the *terminus ad quem*.

There are connections between James and other books of the New Testament, notably I Peter, but we cannot be sure as to whether James used them or they used James.

There are no definite allusions in the Epistle to any particular historical situation. The Epistle is primarily ethical rather than doctrinal. Some have argued from this fact that it was written towards the end of the first or in the second century, after the alleged waning of the influence of the great theologian Paul. But from the same fact, others have argued, perhaps more convincingly, that the Epistle was written about 45 A.D., before the great doctrinal dispute of Acts 15, before Paul had written any of his epistles. If the Epistle was written to Jewish Christians, which seems to be indicated in the address, an earlier dating is almost demanded, because Christianity seems to have become a purely Gentile movement after the fall of Jerusalem. There are no hints of a highly developed organization or doctrine to call for a late date. We see nothing of the heresies that become so prominent later. The whole picture fits admirably with what we know and would expect of an early Christian community in Palestine. There is much to make us feel that James was the first New Testament book written, about 45 A.D.

Place of Writing and Destination

If James, the brother of Jesus, wrote the Epistle, it was almost certainly written in Jerusalem, as all tradition locates his work there. If we accept a late date, after the destruction of Jerusalem, we have no information whatever.

James 1:1 says, "James, a servant of God and of the Lord Jesus Christ, to the twelve tribes which are scattered abroad, greeting." The twelve tribes as such were not in existence in Christian times, but James probably used the expression to refer to the Jews. Of course, he may have been referring to Christians generally as the spiritual Israel; this interpretation is almost forced on those who would date the Epistle late. If it was written to the Jews, it is clear that it was written to Christian Jews.

A probable conclusion is that James the brother of the Lord, the head of the Jerusalem Church, wrote this Epistle about 45 A.D. to all the Christian Jews who were scattered throughout the dispersion.

Contents

This Epistle is much like a sermon, like the wisdom literature of the Old Testament, like the Cynic-Stoic diatribe. The author gives practical advice for the problems of every-day life, problems that were important in the first century and are just as important today. We are not told so much about how to become Christians as how to live as Christians; sanctification rather than justification is the main theme.

The contents do not follow any clear outline, but the following may be suggested:

I. *Christians and persecution, 1:1-27.* Persecution will come, but the Christian will endure it patiently, looking for the fulfilment of the promises.

II. *Christians and respect of persons, 2:1-13.* God does not show partiality; neither should Christians.

III. *Faith and works, 2:14-26.* Faith is not a matter of the intellect alone; a true saving faith produces good works.

IV. *Christians and their tongues, 3:1-18.* The tongue, a little but important member, must be used carefully.

V. *The Christian and the world, 4:1 - 5:6.* God is to be our master rather than Satan.

VI. *Miscellaneous injunctions, 5:7-20.* Be patient. Do not swear. Pray for the sick. Confess your sins. Turn the sinner from his sin.

I Peter

Authorship

The Epistle begins, "Peter, an apostle of Jesus Christ, to the strangers scattered throughout Pontus, Galatia, Cappadocia, Asia, and Bithynia." The Epistle is not anonymous, but claims definitely to have been written by the well-known Apostle Peter. The question, then, is: did Peter really write it, or was it written, probably much later, by someone else and falsely assigned to Peter? Very few try to defend the anonymous theory by thinking of the introduction and conclusion as interpolations; such criticism is entirely subjective and without any basis in fact.

There are certain hints in the Epistle that fit in well with the Petrine authorship. From time to time he makes incidental references to the life of Jesus, which would have been most natural for Peter. In 5:1 he calls himself a "witness of the sufferings of Christ." In 5:13 he calls Mark his son; early tradition is unanimous that Mark was a close companion of Peter, so it is most natural for Peter to have spoken of him as his spiritual son. In 5:12, he calls his scribe, Silvanus, " a faithful brother"; this may have been Paul's companion, who could have helped Peter, probably in Rome. 5:5, "Gird yourselves with humility," may be an allusion to Jesus' washing the disciples' feet. 5:2, "Feed the flock of God," reminds us of the incident by the Sea of Galilee in John 21.

Irenaeus, about 185, was the first known author to assign the Epistle to Peter. In *Against Heresies*, 4, 19, he quotes I Peter 1:8 with the introduction, "Peter says in the Epistle." In 4, 28, he introduces another quotation with "Peter says." Peter is given credit for the Epistle, likewise, by Tertullian and Clement of Alexandria, about 200 A.D., and by many of the Fathers after them. Peter's name is the only one mentioned by any of the Fathers.

Some objections, however, have been raised against the Petrine authorship.

The Greek of the Epistle is unusually good and idiomatic. Could an ignorant Galilean fisherman have produced it? Let us remember that Palestine was bilingual; Peter may have been able to have used good Greek, especially after having been one of the leading apostles for some thirty years. Then 5:12 says that the Epistle was written "through Silvanus." Some think that that means only that Silvanus was the messenger who carried the Epistle, but most believe that such an expression indicates that he was at least the scribe if not the editor. We know enough about stenographers today — to say nothing of editors — to know that they have quite a bit of responsibility for the literary products. The good Greek is no valid argument against Peter's authorship.

The Epistle assumes that the recipients were suffering for their Christianity. It is asserted that that fact proves that the Epistle could not have been written before the time of Domitian, long after Peter's death. If this late date be correct, then Peter cannot have been the author. We shall soon see some reasons for not taking the late date, which will serve to nullify this point.

Another objection is that the Epistle contains too much Pauline thought; the chief apostle would not have borrowed from a secondary apostle, his old enemy. There is the same general theological background, but it is by no means certain that Paul was the only one to hold such beliefs; Conservatives believe that such beliefs go back to the historic Jesus rather than to just Paul. Then this objection makes entirely too much of the supposed hostility between Peter and Paul. The old Tubingen theory has long been exploded. Peter and Paul had differences, but they could differ as Christians and still be good friends. Early tradition has Peter and Paul working together in Rome. Then Peter's scribe may well have been Paul's friend and companion, Silvanus, or Silas. The similarity with Pauline thought is not a bit more than could have reasonably been expected of Peter.

Some assert that the Epistle does not give enough facts about the life of Jesus to have been written by one of His disciples. On the other hand, II Peter makes more use of such facts, and the objectors say that that proves that the author was not Peter but was someone who was definitely feigning to be Peter. It is impossible to please everybody. In fact, neither argument proves a thing; Peter could tell about Jesus when the occasion demanded, but on different occasions he could assume that his readers knew at least the essential facts.

Some object to the Petrine authorship because it is not stated in tradition until Irenaeus, about 185. That is fairly late, but not unreasonably so for a short epistle. But the tradition is unanimous. Then, too, the Epistle was freely used from the end of the first century on, showing that the earliest Fathers considered it authoritative, and no other name beside Peter's has been suggested to account for that authority.

The positive evidence is strong and the negative is weak, so most scholars, even Radical ones, believe that the Apostle Peter wrote the Epistle. If he did not, no one knows who did.

Date

If Peter did write the Epistle, it was, of course, written before his death. We have evidence for the martyrdom of Peter as early as Clement of Rome, about 96. In his letter to the Corinthians, 5:2-4 and 6:1, he tells that Peter was a martyr, and the suggestion is that he, like Paul, was martyred in Rome. Tertullian, about 200, wrote definitely[4]: "Nero first laid bloody hands upon the rising faith at Rome. Then was Peter girded by another when he was bound to the cross." A little later Origen said[5]: "At the end Peter being at Rome was crucified head-downwards, having himself requested that he might so suffer." Eusebius goes to great length to prove Peter's martyrdom under Nero.[6] Tacitus[7] says that great multitudes of the Christians were put to death by Nero in the persecution of 64; he almost certainly died before the death of Nero in 68.

---

4 **Scorpiace**, 15.
5 In Eusebius, **Church History**, 3, 1.
6 **Church History**, 2, 25.
7 **Annals**, 15, 44.

There are literary connections between I Peter and other books of the New Testament that must be considered. There are many striking points of contact with Romans and some with Ephesians and James. Yet it is impossible to be certain as to who used whom. Some use this to date the Epistle after Romans, about 56, or Ephesians, about 61.

When we try to trace the use of I Peter by the Fathers, the matter is similar. There is rather strong evidence that it was used by Clement of Rome in his Epistle to the Corinthians, 96 A.D. Polycarp, 115 A.D., certainly used it. Whether Peter wrote it or not, it must be dated in the first century or the very early second.

Several passages in the Epistle, such as 1:6-7, 2:19-25, and 3:13-17, that tell us that the recipients of the letter were having to suffer for their faith, are to be noted. Some use them to draw the conclusion that the Epistle could not have been written until about 96, the time of the persecution under Domitian that is the background of the Book of Revelation. It is true that we have no evidence of a systematic persecution in Asia Minor until then, but it is by no means certain that such a systematic persecution is back of I Peter. In Revelation we see clearly the demand that the Christians worship the image of the Emperor, and the hostility between Rome and the Church is vividly marked. It is quite different in I Peter; he urges them to submit themselves to the state in 2: 13-17. Nero persecuted the Christians in Rome after the great fire of 64, and it is quite probable that throughout the Empire sporadic uprisings against the Christians may have taken place; this could easily account for the persecution background here, or even the regular persecution to which the Christians were nearly always subject in early times.

A date of 64 or 65 is rather probable. That allows the Petrine authorship, the use of James, Romans, and

Ephesians, the background of the Neronic persecution, and Peter's death under Nero.

Destination and Place of Writing

I Peter 1: 1, 2: "Peter, an apostle of Jesus Christ, to the strangers scattered throughout Pontus, Galatia, Cappadocia, Asia, and Bithynia. Elect according to the foreknowledge of God." These districts are in the northern part of what we know as Asia Minor. The word translated "scattered" means, literally, "of the dispersion," and from this fact some have felt that Peter wrote primarily to the Jews. But the technical dispersion may not have been meant; or Peter may have been using the figure of the spiritual Israel. There may have been some Jewish Christians in these districts at this time, but certain hints in the Epistle make us feel that Peter was thinking primarily of Gentile Christians; e.g., 1:14, 18; 2:9, 10; and 4:3.

5: 13: "The church that is at Babylon, elected together with you, saluteth you; and so doth Marcus my son." The literal city of Babylon in Mesopotamia was in existence at this time and may possibly have been the city from which the Epistle was written. But we know that the Book of Revelation uses Babylon as a symbolic name for Rome, so that from the very earliest times interpreters have felt that Peter was using it in the same symbolic sense. He would not want it too generally known that he was in Rome if the Neronic persecutions against the Christians were going on at the time. We have seen the early tradition that Peter met his death in Rome shortly after this. Rome most easily accounts for Paul's friends, Mark and Silvanus. And a messenger from Rome might easily have taken ship to Pontus, started southwest, circled around the provinces in the order named, and taken ship again in Bithynia or back at Pontus; such a reasonable reconstruction is not possible from the literal Babylon. It may be assumed as fairly certain that the Epistle was written at Rome. It may be that it was Peter's wife at Rome, rather than the church at Rome, that sent salutations, as there are no words in the Greek for the "church that is."

An Outline of the Contents

I Peter is a beautiful, practical little epistle. The readers are urged to be so full of the Christian hope of a glorious immortality that they will be able to live noble Christian lives even in the face of persecution.

I. *The Christians' privileges, 1:1-25.* They have been chosen by God and born of God. They have been redeemed by Jesus Christ. They are to receive an incorruptible inheritance in heaven.

II. *The Christians' duties, 2:1 - 4:11.* Many practical injunctions are given to guide the Christian in his every-day contacts of life. Above all, have fervent love among yourselves.

III. *The Christians' trials, 4: 12-19.* The Christian must expect to suffer as Christ did, but those who suffer with Him will be glorified with Him.

IV. *The Christians' humility, 5: 1-14.* Submit to God and to those whom He has placed over you.

The Life of the Author

Peter was one of the chief apostles, one of the inner circle of three. He was most prominent throughout the gospels and Acts and even the Pauline epistles. Some of the most trustworthy traditions about him have already been mentioned. He was a most interesting and challenging character. He failed often, but he was one of the greatest heroes of the faith.

II Peter

Authorship

1: 1: "Simon Peter, a servant and an apostle of Jesus Christ, to them that have obtained like precious faith with us." The Epistle was written by the Apostle Peter, or it was pseudonymous. There is no doubt as to who the reputed writer was. Besides this verse, the writer claims to have been with Jesus on the Mount of Transfiguration, 1: 16-18, and refers to Jesus' prediction of his death, 1: 14, which probably refers to John 21. Interpolation theories are not used to get rid of the Petrine authorship; either Peter wrote it or whoever wrote it gave him credit for it.

The earliest patristic evidence to the authorship comes from Origen, in the middle of the third century[8]: "Peter left one acknowledged epistle; let there be also a second, for it is disputed." Origen seems to think that Peter wrote II Peter, but he reports doubt. Firmilian, in his letter to Cyprian (No. 75), wrote: ". . . the blessed apostles, Peter and Paul, . . . who in their letters condemned the heretics"; this fits II Peter but hardly I Peter. Eusebius, about 325, places II Peter in his class of books that were disputed but accepted by the majority, rather than in the rejected list[9]; he also says[10]: "The opinion has been handed down to us that the so-called Second Epistle is not canonical, but it has been studied along with the other Scriptures, as it appears profitable to many." Jerome later wrote[11]: "He (Peter) wrote two epistles, which are called catholic; the second of which is denied by very many because of the difference in style between it and the first epistle." As far back as tradition goes, and that is not very early,

8 In Eusebius, **Church History**, 6, 25, 8.
9 **Church History**, 3, 25, 2.
10 **Church History**, 3, 3.
11 **Illustrious Men**, 1.

Peter's name is attached to the Epistle, but doubt is expressed. No name other than Peter's is mentioned.

Many objections have been raised to the Petrine authorship. Some have felt that the writer tries too hard to make himself seem to be Peter. Instead of bringing in incidental memories of the life of Jesus, he makes a point of bringing in the story of the transfiguration and the prophecy of his death. The salutation is more elaborate than I Peter: "Simon Peter, a slave and apostle . . ." All of this is, however, largely a matter of feeling; some feel that Peter would not have written thus; others feel that everything is perfectly natural. I Peter at least makes much of the sayings of Jesus; and the additions in the salutation of II Peter are "Simon" and "slave" rather than the more important words, "Peter" and "apostle."

From the time of Jerome, many have felt that the Epistle was too different in style from I Peter to have been written by the same author. The same argument was used to separate the Fourth Gospel from Revelation. There is a marked difference. I Peter is very smooth, idiomatic Greek, approaching Classical standards of excellence. The style of the second Epistle is clumsy; long sentences are frequently used, but the construction is often cumbersome and the meaning far from clear. Many words are used in the second Epistle that are not found in the first, and many that are not found anywhere else in the New Testament. There is a difficulty here, but not an insuperable one. We are practically certain that Silvanus was the scribe of I Peter; no scribe is mentioned in II Peter. If Peter had no scribe or a different scribe for II Peter, the differences are no greater than might have been expected; a good linguist could change the style of II Peter and make it that of I Peter without great difficulty. The many strange words of II Peter may be accounted for by the different subject-matter; his description of the heretics is quite unique.

3: 2 refers to the words spoken by "your apostles," following the text of the best manuscripts; 3: 4 says: ". . . since the fathers fell asleep." It is asserted that these verses show that the author belonged to a generation when the apostles and the Christian fathers were no longer living. But Peter could have spoken of himself as one of "your apostles," and could have been referring to the words that they had already spoken. "The fathers" who had died before the writing of the Epistle could have been the many older Christians who had died before Peter did, or they could have even been Old Testament saints.

3: 15, 16: ". . . even as our beloved brother Paul also according to the wisdom given him hath written unto you; as also in all his epistles, speaking in them of these things; in which are some things hard to be understood, which they that are unlearned and unstable wrest, as they do also the other scriptures, unto their own destruction." Paul had written some epistles; they had been considered on a par with the Old Testament Scriptures; they had suffered at the hands of false interpreters. Radical critics say that here we have conclusive proof that II Peter was not written until well into the second century, long after the death of Peter, after the concept of an inspired New Testament had arisen. It is true that we do not know of any formal discussion of a New Testament canon until the latter part of the second century, but that by no means proves that the various books were not considered inspired until then. If, as Conservative critics believe, the books are really inspired, they were inspired from the beginning, and that inspiration could have been recognized. Radical criticism needs time to account for the evolution of a belief in inspiration for books that it does not consider inspired; Conservative criticism has no such gap to bridge. A collection of Pauline letters is mentioned, but that does not prove a very late date. The collection need not have been our complete Pauline canon but may have been a smaller group. But even so, many or all of our Pauline letters could have been collected during Peter's lifetime; the death of Paul may have been the occasion of the collection; or if we date Acts about 61, this publication of Paul's life may have been the occasion of the collection of his letters. The Pauline letters were misinterpreted, but again we fail to find positive proof of a late date; false interpretations could have arisen any time after the letters were written.

Chapter two makes a strong attack against a definite type of heresy, the sensual branch of the Gnostic heresy. Some say that this was not in existence until some time in the second century, after Peter's death. It is true that we do not know much about the early history of Gnosticism, but there are at least certain hints that it was under way soon after the middle of the first century. The heresy fought against in Colossians in the early sixties looks very much like an early form of Gnosticism. If the Pastoral Epistles are Pauline, we have more evidence of Gnosticism before Peter's death. We certainly get a very similar picture in the Nicolaitanes of the letters in Revelation some thirty years after the time of Peter's death. It is unsafe to say that the heresy of II Peter 2 could not have arisen before Peter's death.

There is a very close connection between Jude and II Peter, especially chapter 2. The general theme is the same; many of the same illustrations from the Old Testament are found in both; there is even a high degree of verbal similarity. It is impossible to be absolutely sure as to which was written first, though most scholars favor the priority of Jude. If the author of II Peter used Jude, and if Jude was written after Peter's death, Peter could not have written II Peter. But we cannot be sure about either of the *if* clauses. II Peter and Jude may even have been written at the same time and place.

The Petrine authorship has certainly been strongly opposed from early times, and we would do well to refrain from dogmatism today. The Conservative cannot consider any one of the negative proofs as absolutely final, though he must admit that many straws come to have considerable weight. Some Conservatives believe that II Peter 1:1 is absolute proof that Peter wrote it. Possibly so; but it is interesting to notice that that did not settle it for the early Church Fathers; nor did not keep even such a man as John Calvin[12] from having grave doubts. Why, especially, was the Church so slow in accepting it if it was written by Peter? Possibly because it was so short that it was unnoticed for a time; some have suggested that it may have been written to Jews and that the later Gentile Christians did not care much for it for that reason. We do not know. We can say that we believe more or less strongly that Peter wrote it, but that is about as far as we should go. What shall we do if we believe that Peter did not write it? Some would say that that would mean that we should not include it in the canonical New Testament but put it with the pseudonymous gospels, acts, epistles, and revelations of the second and later centuries. Possibly so; though we shall probably never get our New Testaments printed without it. Some say that we should still leave it in the canon, considering it as giving the true apostolic teaching, and thinking that the

---

12 Calvin, in his introduction to his commentary on II Peter concludes his discussion thus: "But since it is not quite evident as to the author, I shall allow myself the liberty of using the word Peter or Apostle indiscriminately."

author meant nothing dishonest by his claim in 1: 1, but that he was using a device common to the literary practice of his day. Pseudonymous books were very common from the second century on, and at least some were produced before the Christian era. Probably most Conservatives will continue to hold rather tentatively to the Petrine authorship.

Date

If Peter wrote the Epistle, he wrote it before his death, which, as we have seen above, took place between about 64 and 68. 1: 14 indicates that he was expecting his death soon. 3: 1 calls this the second epistle, so it was probably written after I Peter, though some few think that he was referring to an earlier, lost letter, and that I Peter came last. On the basis of the Petrine authorship, 67 or shortly before is the best date.

Most of the objections to the Petrine authorship point to a second-century or later date, so if Peter did not write it, we should probably place it somewhere in the second century. The Epistle is so short and is so much like Jude that it is impossible to be sure as to when the Fathers began to use it. There are rather strong hints of it in the middle of the second century, but we cannot be absolutely sure of its use until the time of Origen. About 150 is about as good a guess as we can make on the non-Petrine theory.

Destination and Place of Writing

1: 1 says simply, "Simon Peter . . . to them that have obtained like precious faith with us through the righteousness of God and our Saviour Jesus Christ." 3: 1 says that this is the second epistle, so if the first was I Peter, as is most probable, this letter must have been addressed also to those Christians in the northern part of Asia Minor, to those provinces named in I Peter

1: 1. Of course, if the letter was not written by Peter, or if the first epistle referred to in 3: 1 was not I Peter, we can say simply that it was sent to some Christians somewhere.

The author does not say where he was when he wrote. On the basis of the Petrine authorship, Rome is the most probable place of writing, as the author seems to be expecting his death soon (1: 14), and seemingly trustworthy tradition says that he was killed in Rome. The case for Rome is even stronger if I Peter was written before II Peter and the Babylon of I Peter 5: 13 is Rome. We know nothing in favor of any place other than Rome.

An Outline of the Contents

The chapter divisions indicate rather accurately the divisions of thought.

I. *Grow in grace, chapter 1.* The Christian should make progress, using all the means of grace for growth in Godliness, especially God's own revelation in Scripture.

II. *Avoid false teachings, chapter 2.* There have always been those who have misinterpreted Scripture. Their false doctrine will destroy them, and it will destroy you if you follow them.

III. *Remember the promise of the Second Coming of Jesus, chapter 3.* Many are mockingly denying that He is coming again, but God always keeps His promises. In God's own time, the Day of the Lord will come, striking terror to the hearts of the ungodly and bringing eternal bliss to those that are His. The fact that our Lord may come at any time should make all Christians live beautiful lives, so that they will not be ashamed when He comes.

The Heresy of II Peter 2 and Jude

Many details make us feel certain that we are dealing with a branch of the Gnostic heresy. The heretics claimed to have a secret knowledge (*gnosis*), which they expressed in mysterious, high-sounding language. Matter and spirit were widely separated; matter was considered bad and spirit good. Some men were material; some spiritual. A spiritual God could not have created the material universe, so God was separated from the creator. A highly fantastic system of intermediaries between God and the universe was developed. Jesus was not considered as the true God-man. Such were some of the principal beliefs of the Gnostics.

Beliefs influence actions. The belief that matter is entirely evil led the Gnostics to take wrong attitudes toward their bodies. Some went to the extreme of asceticism; our bodies are bad, so let us punish them and subdue them and do nothing that will give them pleasure. Others went to exactly the opposite extreme; our bodies are evil, so it makes no difference what we do with them; we can indulge in any sensual lusts without affecting our spirits; let us indulge in these lusts and show our contempt for our bodies. Sensualism is more popular than asceticism; so in II Peter and Jude it is the sensualists who are most prominent.

Gnosticism struck at the heart of the Christian faith and morality. It called for utter condemnation on the part of those who were true Christians, and Peter and Jude do not spare words in doing this. The Nicolaitanes of Revelation 2 and 3, almost certainly some of the Gnostics, come in for terrific condemnation there.

Gnosticism proved very popular in certain quarters. It began in New Testament times. It became very important in the history of the early Church. The Fathers finally won out in their fight against it. Gnosticism as such is gone, but many of its beliefs and beliefs similar to them are still with us, and the Church still has the duty of preserving and defending "the faith which was once delivered to the saints."

JUDE

Authorship

The Epistle claims to have been written by "Jude, the servant of Jesus Christ, and brother of James." Jude, or Judas, and James were two of the most common names. "The servant of Jesus Christ" means a Christian. There may have been many Christians named Jude with brothers James. But the fact that the author does not further identify himself or his brother makes us think that one or both may have been well known. We think immediately of James the brother of Jesus, the head of the early Jerusalem church, and his brother Jude, mentioned in Mk. 6: 3 and Mt. 13:55. That would, of course, make Jude the brother of Jesus, which he does not claim to be. The author of the Epistle of James claimed to be only "a servant of God and of the Lord Jesus Christ." In both cases modesty may have made them refrain from claiming Jesus as their brother. In Luke 6: 16 and Acts 1: 13, in the list of apostles, we have a Judas the son of James. In the Greek there are no words for "the son"; we have simply the genitive of relationship, which is most often used of the relationship between parent and child but which can be used of any other relationship. The apostolic Jude may have been the brother of some James. The brothers of Jesus seem to have been antagonistic to Him until after the resurrection, so these two Judes, are probably not to be identified. There are other Judes, but these two are the only ones about whom we know who may have had a brother James. One of these two or some other unknown Jude may have written the Epistle, or the Epistle may have been pseudonymous.

Tertullian and the Latin version of Origen call Jude an apostle, which lends some weight to the view that he was one of the twelve; but we must remember that the term apostle had a wider use, James the brother of Jesus having been called an apostle by Paul. The Fathers from 200 on mention the Epistle and its author but add nothing to the information we get from the Epistle itself. Origen mentioned the fact that some doubted the authority of the Epistle, and Eusebius put it in his class of books that were disputed but accepted by most.

Some think that there are certain hints in the Epistle which prove that it was written by a Christian of the second generation, or even later, rather than by either of the better known Judes. Vs. 3 speaks of the "faith which was once delivered to the saints," which is at best a mere suggestion, not a proof. Vs. 17, "remember ye the words which were spoken before of the apostles," is a weak suggestion that the writer was not an apostle himself and that he belonged to a later generation. The type of heresy denounced is claimed as evidence for a second-century date, but we have seen in connection with II Peter that we cannot be sure of that. The doubt recorded by the Fathers indicates that some in the Church doubted that it was written by either of the more famous Judes.

The evidence for the authorship is by no means conclusive for any one. Jude the brother of Jesus and James seems most probable. The Jewish tone of the Epistle is what we should expect from him. The doubt as to its acceptance may have been wholly due to the fact that it quotes from an apocryphal book, Enoch, with the introduction "Enoch . . . prophesied." That does raise the question of the canonicity of Enoch, but does not prove that the author considered it inspired; the Biblical use of "prophecy" is very broad.

Date

Nothing is known from the New Testament or from any trustworthy tradition as to the death of either Jude. A passage in Hegesippus about the grandsons of Judas the brother of Jesus suggests that Judas was dead before the time of Domitian, but there is nothing certain. Either Jude must have died in the first century.

Jude seems to have been earlier than II Peter from the literary relationships, though some scholars favor the opposite view. Unless the heresy denounced is considered too late, there is no real reason for not dating Jude in the early sixties, probably between I and II Peter, about 65.

If we do not take this earlier dating and think of one of the earlier Judes as the author, there is nothing to give a certain date. Literary allusions do not become definite until the third century. Those who favor a later date usually place it just a little earlier than their late date for II Peter, a little before 150.

Destination and Place of Writing

We really know nothing of either of these. The address is most general: "to them that are sanctified by God the Father, and preserved in Jesus Christ, and called"; that is, to Christians. It may have been a truly general letter, though it may have been sent to some section that is not now known. From the allusions to the Gnostic heresy in Colossians, the Pastorals, II Peter, and Revelation, it seems that Asia Minor was at least one definite center of the heresy. It may be that Jude was sent to some part of Asia Minor, too.

The fact that Jude is so much like II Peter, which probably came from Rome, makes Rome a likely place for the composition of Jude. Jerusalem too may be considered as a possibility because of the Jewish allusions and the established connection of James with Jerusalem. But nothing can be considered at all certain.

Contents

As the Epistle contains only one chapter, no attempt will be made to outline it. The Epistle opens with a salutation, states the purpose of the letter, gives a condemnation of the Gnostic heresy, reminds the readers of some of their Christian duties, and closes with a beautiful doxology.

XII

THE JOHANNINE LITERATURE

THE literature that has been traditionally assigned to the Apostle John includes all the types of literature that are found in the New Testament: historical, the Fourth Gospel; epistolary, I, II, and III John, and prophetic, the Apocalypse, or Revelation.

AUTHORSHIP

The question of the authorship of the different books in the Johannine literature is one of the most interesting and complicated that New Testament criticism has before itself today. It is also a question of considerable importance: if the Apostle John wrote the Fourth Gospel, then the testimony of that Gospel is that of an eyewitness, one of the most intimate companions of Jesus.

Before we go further, it may be well to realize, however, that anyone can attack this problem without fear of having to give up any theory he may have as to the inspiration or authority of the Bible. Even if we accept all of the Johannine books as the work of one author, and that may not be necessary, there is nothing in any of them that definitely states that their author was the Apostle John, the son of Zebedee. The Fourth Gospel claims that it was written by "the disciple whom Jesus loved." The second and third epistles claim to have been written by "the elder." The author of Revelation calls himself "John." Putting all these together, we would get only John, the beloved disciple, the elder; and such a person need not definitely be identified with the Apostle John, the son of Zebedee. If, after reviewing all the evidence we have at hand, we arrive at the conclusion that the Apostle John did not write one, or any, of these books, we may still believe in all of them as inspired and authoritative.

Scholars are divided into three schools of thought on this subject: some think that the Apostle John wrote all five books; some think that he did not write any of them; and some think that he wrote some but not all of them.

I. Evidence of Apostolic Authorship

A. External Evidence

1. *The Gospel.* The existence of the Gospel is recognized as early as Ignatius and Polycarp, about 110 A.D. These and others after them use the Gospel, but no one mentions the name of the author until Theophilus, Bishop of Antioch. About 180 he wrote[1]: "The Holy Scripture teaches us, and all the inspired writers, one of whom, John, says, 'In the beginning was the Word, and the Word was with God . . .' "

Irenaeus (about 190), who had lived in his youth with the friend and disciple of John, Polycarp, writes as follows:[2] "Matthew published his gospel-writing among the Hebrews in their own language, while Peter and Paul were in Rome preaching the gospel and founding the Church. After their decease, Mark, the disciple and interpreter of Peter, also wrote and transmitted to us what Peter had preached, while Luke, the attendant of Paul, recorded in a book the gospel preached by Paul. Afterwards John the disciple of the Lord, who

[1] To Autolycus, 1, 13.
[2] Against Heresies, 3, 1; Eusebius, C. H., 5. 8, 2-3.

also reclined on His bosom, published the gospel while he was residing at Ephesus in Asia." Irenaeus mentions in several places this sojourn of John in Asia, and says that John lived until the time of Trajan, who came to the throne in 98. Irenaeus makes no fewer than five hundred quotations from the four gospels, one hundred of these being from the Fourth Gospel.

Clement of Alexandria, about 200, says[3]: "John, the last, having noticed that the bodily things were recorded in the (first three) gospels, at the instigation of men of note, and moved by the Spirit, composed a spiritual gospel." Clement quotes the gospels hundreds of times and frequently cites John's by name.

Tertullian, about 200, left abundant testimony to the existence and apostolic authority of each of the gospels. He cites passages from almost every chapter of the Fourth Gospel, and from some chapters almost every verse.

The following note about the Fourth Gospel comes from the Muratorian Fragment, which probably originated in Italy between 170 and 200: "The Fourth Gospel is by John. John, one of the disciples, being solicited by his fellow-disciples and bishops, said to them, 'Let us fast together for the next three days, and then communicate to each other the revelations which each shall have received.' The following night it was revealed to Andrew, one of the Apostles, that John should write the whole in his own name, and that all the others should criticise what he had written. . . . What is there, then, surprising in the fact that John should say in his epistles, speaking himself, 'That which we have heard, which we have seen with our eyes, and our hands have handled . . . declare we unto you.' He thus proclaims himself to be not only an eye and

---

[3] Eusebius, C. H., 6, 14, 7.

ear witness, but also the narrator of all the wonderful events of the Lord's life."

Origen, about 250, says[4]: "Last of all that by John. . . . Why need we speak of him who reclined upon the bosom of Jesus, John, who has left us one gospel, though he confessed that he might write so many that the world could not contain them? He wrote also the Apocalypse, but was commanded to keep silence and not to write the words of the seven thunders. And he has left also an epistle of very few lines; perhaps also a second and third; but not all consider them genuine, and together they do not contain a hundred lines."

Eusebius, about 325, says[5]: "The three gospels previously written having come into general circulation and also having been handed to John, they say that he admitted them, giving his testimony to their truth; but alleging that there was wanting in the narration the account of the things done by Christ at the commencement of His ministry. And this was the truth; for it is evident that the other three evangelists only wrote the deeds of our Lord one year after the imprisonment of John the Baptist, and intimated this in the very beginning of their history. . . . One who understands this can no longer think that the gospels are at variance with one another, inasmuch as the Gospel according to John contains the first acts of Christ, while the others give an account of the latter part of His life."

A Latin manuscript, Toletanus, though written in the tenth century, preserves a tradition that seems to be earlier than a similar one in Jerome, so that it may be considered as coming from the third or fourth century: "The Apostle John, whom the Lord Jesus loved

[4] In Eusebius, C. H., 6, 25, 6-10.
[5] C. H., 3, 24, 7-13.

most, last of all wrote this gospel, at the request of the bishops of Asia. . . . This gospel, it is manifest, was written after the Apocalypse, and was given to the churches in Asia by John while he was yet in the body; as Papias, bishop of Hierapolis, a disciple of John and dear to him, related in his *Exoterica*, at the end of the five books." If this is a correct quotation from Papias (about 125-140 A.D.), this becomes our earliest testimony as to the authorship of any of the Johannine books.

2. *Revelation.* Other than the testimony given above from Papias, the earliest testimony for the authorship of Revelation is that of Justin, about 152-160, who says[6]: "John, one of the apostles of the Christ, in the Apocalypse . . ."

Irenaeus, about 190, calls the author of the Gospel and Revelation "the disciple of the Lord."[7]

Hippolytus, from 204 to 235, frequently calls the author John, calling him both apostle and disciple.

Tertullian, 197 - 222, frequently quotes from the Apocalypse, and he calls it the work of the Apostle John.[8]

The passage quoted above from Origen calls the Apostle John the author of Revelation as well as the Gospel.

3. *The Epistles.* There are echoes and influences of the Epistles as early as the time of Clement of Rome (about 95) and Polycarp (about 115), but we do not find the author named until we come to Irenaeus (about 185)[9]: "John, the disciple of the Lord, . . . has thus testified to us in his Epistle: 'Little children, it is the last time; and as ye have heard that Anti-

---

6 Dialogue, 81.
7 3, 2, 1 ff; 4, 20, 11.
8 Marc. 3, 14, 24.
9 3, 16, 5.

christ doth come, now have many antichrists appeared . . .' " His quotation includes I John 2:18, 19, 21, 22. In 3, 16, 8, he quotes from II John 7, 8 as from the Epistle already mentioned.

Clement of Alexandria, about 200, quotes frequently from the First Epistle and recognizes that there are at least two Epistles: in *Str*. 2, 15, 66, he quotes from "John's greater epistle."

The Muratorian Canon, probably between 170 and 200, speaks of "John in his Epistles," and "two epistles of John."

The quotation given above from Origen mentions the First Epistle and "perhaps also a second and third, but not all consider them genuine."

Tertullian, about 200, frequently quotes from the First Epistle by name and probably uses the Second; there seems to be no trace of the Third.

Eusebius, about 325, calls the First Epistle John's, and places it in his "accepted" list. The Second and Third are placed in the "disputed" list, "whether they be by the Evangelist, or by another of the same name."[10]

B. *Internal Evidence*

John 21:20-24: "Then Peter, turning about, seeth the disciple whom Jesus loved following; which also leaned on his breast at supper, and said, Lord, which is he that betrayeth thee? Peter seeing him saith to Jesus, Lord, and what shall this man do? Jesus saith unto him, If I will that he tarry till I come, what is that to thee? Follow thou me. Then went this saying abroad among the brethren, that that disciple should not die; yet Jesus said not unto him, He shall not die; but, if I will that he tarry till I come, what is that to thee? This is the disciple which testifieth of these things, and wrote these things: and we know that his

[10] C. H., 3, 25, 2-3.

testimony is true." As the Gospel clearly closes with chapter 20, chapter 21 is evidently a postscript or appendix. Judging by its style, it was probably written by the author of the Gospel. Probably the statement "and we know that his testimony is true" is not the work of the author. But even if the whole of the 21st chapter be not the work of the author, at least it is extremely early testimony and therefore valuable. The author is said to be "the disciple whom Jesus loved." This disciple is particularly prominent during the closing scenes of the Gospel. He was present at the Last Supper. He stood by the foot of the cross, and the Virgin Mary was entrusted to his care. He brought Peter into the High Priest's palace and accompanied him to the empty tomb. He also figures in the last scene of all, by the shore of the Sea of Galilee.

Revelation claims to have been written by John. 1:1: "The Revelation of Jesus Christ, which God gave him to show unto his servants things which must shortly come to pass; and he sent and signified it by his angel unto his servant John." 1:4: "John to the seven churches which are in Asia." 1:9: "I John, who also am your brother, and companion in tribulation, and in the kingdom and patience of Jesus Christ, was in the isle that is called Patmos." 22:8: "And I John saw these things, and heard them." John was a very common name, but this John was writing to churches that knew him well and knew who "John" meant. This is quite different from what we find in the later pseudonymous books: e.g., "The Apocalypse of the Holy Apostle Paul," and "The Apocalypse of Saint John the Theologue," books written long after Paul and John were dead.

The Second and Third Epistles were written by "the Elder." II John 1: "The elder unto the elect lady and her children." III John 1: "The elder unto the wellbeloved Gaius."

The First Epistle claims to have been written by an eye-witness of the things about which he writes. 1:1-4: "That which was from the beginning, which we have heard, which we have seen with our eyes, which we have looked upon, and our hands have handled, of the Word of life: . . . That which we have seen and heard declare we unto you, that your joy may be full." The Gospel also makes claim of having been written by an eye-witness: 1:4: "And the Word was made flesh and dwelt among us, (and we beheld his glory, the glory as of the only begotten of the Father,) full of grace and truth." 19:35: "And he that saw it bare record, and his record is true: and he knoweth that he saith true, that ye might believe."

Besides these direct claims of authorship, we can get some hints that fit in well with them. The author of the Gospel seems to have been a Palestinian Jew. He was quite familiar with Jewish ideas, customs, and traits. He quotes the Old Testament from the Septuagint and from the Hebrew. His language has a marked Aramaic style, so much so that some men think that it was written in Aramaic and then translated into Greek. The author frequently brings in minute matters of topography of Palestine which in themselves are of no importance but are exactly the kind of detail which would lodge in the mind of an observant eye-witness. The author seems to know the persons whom he describes in a remarkably intimate way; we see his characters walk and talk, and think and feel. Many little details of time, number, and place are found in the Gospel. The author seems to have been closely allied with Jesus. He describes for us the most intimate details of the life of Jesus. The author was familiar with the places where Jesus was accustomed to resort with His disciples. The author was familiar with wrong impressions that had been held by the disciples, which Jesus corrected at the time or later: 2:21, 22: "But he spake of the temple of his body. When therefore he was risen from the dead, his disciples remembered that he had said this unto them." See also 11:13; 12:16; 13:28; 20:9; and 21:4. Then there are a number of passages that can best be explained as the product of an intimate friend of Jesus: 2:24, "But Jesus did not commit himself unto them, because he knew all men." Similarly, 6:6, 15, 61, 64; 7:1; 11:33; 13:1-3, 11, 21; 16:19; 18:4; and 19:28. The author knows the companions of Jesus intimately, and he tells about many of them by name, but he never speaks by name of the apostles John or James. Now we know that Peter, James, and John were the inner circle of disciples, the ones that Jesus seemed to love in a special sense. Peter is mentioned by name time and again all through the Gospel, so he is not to be thought of as the anonymous "disciple whom Jesus loved." James could not have been the author, because we know from Acts 12:2 that he was martyred early, long before the Gospel could have been written. John, the son of Zebedee, is then the natural one to identify as the beloved disciple.

Let us turn, now, to

II. Evidence Against the Apostolic Authorship

A. External Evidence

1. The hesitation of Rome—the Alogoi: Hippolytus, about 200, wrote a defense of the Gospel and Apocalypse of John; a defense implies an attack. From Epiphanius, in the fourth century, we learn that in the latter part of the second century there were some people who rejected the Fourth Gospel, alleging that it was the work of a Gnostic, Cerinthus; Epiphanius calls these the Alogoi. Irenaeus defends the four gospels, implying that some were under attack. The Muratorian fragment on the canon goes out of its way to defend the Fourth Gospel, also implying attack.

2. The silence of Ignatius: Ignatius wrote to Ephesus, where John was supposed to have written the Gospel, less than twenty years after John was supposed to have written it. He mentions the Apostle Paul but not John.

3. The early martyrdom of John:

a. In Mark 10:39, Jesus speaks to James and John: "Ye shall indeed drink of the cup that I drink of; and with the baptism that I am baptized withal shall ye be baptized." (Similarly, Matt. 20:23.) Many of those who take the Radical view of prophecy infer from this that both James and John had already suffered martyrdom before the Gospel of Mark had been written.

b. Papias' statement: George Hamartolos, a ninth century writer, says that Papias says in his second book that John "was killed by the Jews, thus plainly fulfilling, along with his brother, the prophecy of Christ regarding them and their own confession and common agreement concerning him." The De Boor fragment, a seventh or eighth century work, says: "Papias in his second book says that John the divine and James his brother were killed by the Jews."

c. The testimony of the Church calendars: In the fourth-century Syriac calendar, "John and James, the apostles in Jerusalem," are commemorated together as martyrs there on Dec. 27, between Stephen (Dec. 26) and Paul and Peter (in Rome, Dec. 28). Other later calendars agree.

d. Aphrahat, about 344, writes[11]: "Great and ex-

---

[11] **De Persecutione, 23.**

cellent is the martyrdom of Jesus . . . and after Him was the faithful martyr . . . Simon also and Paul were perfect martyrs. And James and John walked in the footsteps of Christ, their Master."

e. Herakleon, about 125, the early Gnostic commentator on the Fourth Gospel, in listing those who had escaped martyrdom, omits the name of John.[12]

4. *Possible confusion of two Johns.* The Apostle John may have come to have been confused with another John, who may have been the author of the Gospel. Papias, about 140, quoted by Eusebius, says[13]: "And again, on any occasion when a person came who had been a follower of the Elders, I would enquire about the discourses of the Elders,—what was said by Andrew or by Peter, or by Philip, or by Thomas or James, or by John or Matthew or any other of the Lord's disciples, and what Aristion and the Elder John, the disciples of the Lord, say." Papias was born a little after 70. This passage seems to imply that the Apostle John had passed on, but that the Elder John, a disciple of the Lord, was still alive in Papias' youth. Irenaeus, about 185, also writes that Papias "was a hearer of John," and means that he was a hearer of a John who had heard Jesus. After referring to this statement of Irenaeus, Eusebius, about 325, proceeds to show at great length that the John whom Papias heard was not the Apostle John but the other John.

5. *The age of John:* The Gospel is to be dated at the end of the first century, possibly between 90 and 95. If the Apostle John were its author, he would have been, probably, eighty or ninety years old when he wrote.

---

[12] In Clement of Alexandria, Strom. 4, 9.
[13] Eusebius, C. H., 3, 39, 1-7.

B. *Internal Evidence*

1. *The character of the Gospel:* There are some critics who think that the synoptic account of the life of Jesus is to be preferred to that of the Fourth Gospel, that the latter is secondary, and that, therefore, it could not have been the work of an eye-witness. Radical criticism finds it practically impossible to believe that the Apostle John wrote the Gospel because of the way the Gospel treats Jesus. Jesus is presented as the pre-existent Logos, the Messiah, the mighty Miracle Worker, the sinless One, the Son of God, very God Himself. Radical criticism believes in only a human Jesus; how, then, could an intimate companion of a human being ever come to consider him such a figure as we find in the Fourth Gospel?

2. *Son of Thunder — Beloved Disciple:* In the Synoptic Gospels, John and James are called "sons of thunder," Mk. 3:17. In Mk. 10, he and James are asking for the first seats in the Kingdom. In Lk. 9: 51-56, he asks Jesus if He doesn't want to bid fire come from heaven and destroy the Samaritans. Could this son of thunder have been the disciple whom Jesus loved, who leaned upon His breast, who wrote the beautiful Fourth Gospel?

3. *Greek flavor of the Gospel:* Some critics have felt that the Fourth Gospel is too Greek, both in language and thought, to have been written by an Aramaic-speaking fisherman of Galilee.

III. Evidence in Favor of Divided Authorship

A. Difference in style: Dionysius, writing in Alexandria, about 250, called attention to the difference in style between the Gospel and Revelation and drew the conclusion that they could not have been written by the same person. One cannot read the two books in Greek without seeing the difference. The Greek of the Gospel is smooth and regular, while that of Revelation is rough, frequently violating all rules of grammar. The style of the Epistles is like that of the Gospel.

B. The possible confusion of two Johns: We saw above that Eusebius drew the conclusion from Papias that there were two famous Johns, the Apostle and the Elder. Some critics believe that the Elder wrote the Gospel and Epistles and that the Apostle wrote the Apocalypse. Some believe that the Elder wrote the Gospel and Epistles and that an otherwise unknown Prophet John wrote Revelation. Various other combinations are held. Some say that we do not know who wrote any of the books; they can be sure only that the Gospel and Revelation were not written by the same person.

IV. An Evaluation of the Evidence

We see that the Fourth Gospel was in existence from at least the early part of the second century, and it seems to be placed on a par with the other gospels at least by the time of Tatian, about 160. Revelation and at least the First Epistle can be traced back to the earliest part of the second century or the close of the first.

The first writer that we know of who definitely quotes from the Gospel as the work of "John" is Theophilus, though there is a possibility that Papias does in his almost unknown *Exoterica.* Revelation is called John's by Justin. One or more epistles are called John's by Irenaeus. Irenaeus identifies John as "the disciple of the Lord, who also reclined on His bosom." The author is frequently called John, the disciple of the Lord, after this. The Latin manuscript of the fourth century calls him the apostle. Were the earlier writers trying to distinguish a disciple John from the apostle John? Possibly so, but probably not. We know that the word "apostle" was not limited to the twelve, and we know that the twelve were often called "disciples." The earlier writers give not the slightest intimation that they were trying to exclude the Apostle John from being the author.

There is only one discordant note in the testimony of the early Church on the subject of authorship. The "Alogoi," toward the end of the second century, alleged that the Gospel was the work of the Gnostic Cerinthus, although, strange to say, Irenaeus tells us that it was the very object of the Gospel to refute the errors of this Cerinthus, a purpose which it was well fitted to serve by the emphasis which is laid on the reality of the Incarnation. The Alogoi were a very obscure sect, of whom only one supporter can be named with any degree of probability, namely, Caius of Rome. The value of the evidence of this little sect against the united evidence of the early Church must be considered small. In a way, we may be thankful for this opposition. It shows that there were critics in the early church. The church did not accept the Johannine writings blindly. They had their opponents, and if those opponents had been able to give any definite proof that these writings could not have been written by the apostle—such, for example, as that the Apostle had been martyred long before the Gospel was written—the belief in the apostolic authorship might have been killed. But they were not able to do this. The "silence of Ignatius" proves nothing. No argument from silence gives absolute proof. This argument from silence does not make even a strong suggestion. Why does he mention Paul and not John in his letter to the Ephesians? Two reasons may be advanced: his letter is full of Pauline thought, and Ignatius was going to Rome facing martyrdom, just as Paul had done. There is no real reason why he should have mentioned John.

If it could be proved that the Apostle John was martyred long before the Johannine books were written, of course he could not have been their author. Judging from the eighth-century De Boor fragment and the ninth-century George Hamartolos, there must have been some statement in Papias that could have been interpreted — or misinterpreted — into the statement that John was killed by the Jews. The place where the Jews were most likely to have had the power and opportunity to kill John was Jerusalem, and Jerusalem was destroyed in 70, which is almost certainly before the Johannine books were written. But that is not the only possibility. Jews were scattered all over the world. The Jews persecuted Paul at Lystra and Thessalonica in Acts; they were the persecutors of the Smyrna Church in Revelation. Nor was the power of the Jews destroyed in 70; the great rebellion under Bar Cochba took place well in the second century. Even if the statement that John was martyred by the Jews is correct, that does not prove early martyrdom. Then there is always the possibility that the writer of the De Boor fragment and George Hamartolos may have misinterpreted Papias — they may have taken *martus*, for example, to have meant "martyr," while Papias may have meant it to mean simply "witness." The Syrian calendar has "John and James, the apostles in Jerusalem," commemorated together as martyrs on Dec. 27. Certainly James and John were not martyred at the same time. If Papias or the calendars imply martyrdom at the same time, they are evidently wrong. The Syrian calendar seems to imply that the martyrdom took place in Jerusalem, which suggests a date before 70. But we cannot be sure that this is a necessary implication or that the calendars had access to accurate information. Then, although we know practically nothing of the history of Jerusalem for many years after its fall, we cannot be certain that John could not have been martyred there on a visit in his old age. The case for the early martyrdom has some very weak links, and the whole thing may have started from a misundertanding.

Eusebius understood the Papias passage to indicate that there were two Johns, an apostle and an elder. Many since the time of Eusebius have used that in favor of divided authorship or of throwing the Apostle entirely out of the picture. The name John is mentioned twice, but in both cases the John is called both disciple and elder; why, then, should we call the first one the apostle and the second the elder? The only difference is that the first mention of John is in a group that "said," while the second mention is in a group that "say." The difference in tense does not necessitate the view of two different Johns; it can well be explained by supposing that the one John, a disciple and an elder, was grouped with the earlier important group and then lived long enough to have been grouped with the second group. Eusebius evidently was accustomed to having trouble in interpreting Papias, as he called him "a remarkably stupid man." The Papias passage is far from clear; it can hardly be said, however, that the case for an Elder John, distinct from the Apostle John, rests on a very firm foundation.

As to the allegation that the Apostle John would have been too old to have been the author of the Johannine books, it is to be said that the Apostle need not have been over eighty or ninety years of age. Of course, that is a rather old age, but it is by no means impossible that such an old man could have produced this literature; we know men that old today that are still active mentally. There are many who feel that the Gospel and the First Epistle, especially, show signs of having been produced by an old man.

The claim that the internal character of the Gospel and its picture of the divine Jesus, the pre-existent Logos, prove that it could not have been written by the Apostle John, the companion of Jesus, means a great deal to a Radical but nothing to a Conservative. The Radical believes that Jesus was only a man, therefore he cannot believe that a close friend of Jesus could have ever pictured him as the Fourth Gospel does. The Conservative has no such difficulty, because he believes that Jesus was just what the Johannine literature says that He was.

The objection that one of the "sons of thunder" could not have been "the disciple whom Jesus loved" carries little weight. Jesus loved the unworthy Peter; he even chose Judas as one of the twelve. And could not a veritable son of thunder who had been influenced by Jesus and His teaching for sixty years have written this beautiful literature?

The statement that the Gospel could not have been written by the Apostle because of its Greek rather than Aramaic style carries little weight now in the light of the recent studies of Burney, Torrey, Montgomery, and Schlatter. These men have detected such a strong Aramaic style that they have suggested that the Gospel may originally have been written in Aramaic and later translated into Greek.

We must admit that there is a marked difference in style between Revelation and the rest of the Johannine group. But does that necessitate the view of difference in authorship? By no means. It is a well-known fact that the New Testament writers made use of scribes; several of them are mentioned by name. Scribes, like modern stenographers, probably had their part in making the final product smooth and grammatical. When John was a prisoner on Patmos, writing Revelation, he surely did not have many scribes to choose from, if he had any at all; Revelation was the product of the Galilean fisherman, possibly aided by a poor scribe. When he was writing the other books, though, he was in Ephesus, an honored dignitary of a large Christian center, and he probably had the services of the best of the scribes. Some feel that the subject-matter and the excitement of Revelation had something to do with its roughness. Some hold to the theory that Revelation was written in the sixties, when John had not learned much Greek, and that the other books were written in the nineties, after he had become more proficient; however, it is practically impossible to date Revelation that early.

The evidence for the apostolic authorship of the Second and Third Epistles is rather weak, but that is probably due, in a measure at least, to their shortness and their personal nature.

Such is the very confused evidence; scholars still differ widely in their conclusions drawn from it. The negative evidence has weight, especially to a Radical; but a Conservative cannot think that this negative evidence is conclusive. While it may be freely admitted that the internal evidence for the apostolic authorship is by no means conclusive, yet it does help out the external evidence we have, and together they make a very convincing case. We must refrain from being too dogmatic, but we can say that the Conservative at least has very good grounds for believing that the Apostle John was the author of all the Johannine literature.

Dates

From the time of Irenaeus on, tradition is unanimous that the Gospel of John was the last of the four, written in Ephesus. John was almost certainly not in Ephesus while Paul was there or when Paul wrote Ephesians or the letters to Timothy. He may have gone to Ephesus after the destruction of Jerusalem in 70. Irenaeus says that John lived on until the time of Trajan, who became emperor in 98. The Gospel seems clearly to have been used by Ignatius about 115, so we cannot place it far into the second century. We cannot be at all certain as to the date, but somewhere in the eighties or nineties seems best. A few scholars who think that the Gospel was written originally in Aramaic date it in the sixties and say that it was written in Palestine, but that whole theory has won very few followers.

Early tradition is almost unanimous in dating Revelation in the last years of Domitian, who reigned from 81 to 96: e.g., Irenaeus, Clement of Alexandria, Origen, and Victorinus. A few later authorities place it in the reigns of Claudius (41-54), or Nero (54-68), or Trajan (98-117). The internal evidence of the book seems to agree best with the Domitianic date. The churches in Asia Minor had been in existence long enough for definite heresy to have arisen and for deterioration to have taken place in some of them. The persecution of the churches by Rome can be accounted for during the reign of Domitian; the persecution of the Christians by Nero seems to have been confined rather closely to Rome. Revelation 13 and 17 mention the popular myth that Nero came to life again after having killed himself; John does not believe this superstition, but he seems to make use of it in the sense that the persecutor Domitian is the reincarnation of the former persecutor, Nero. Rev. 17:10 suggests that the sixth emporer, Vespasian (69-79), was reigning; this particular vision may have come from that time, though that is not the only possible interpretation, but the evidence for the Domitianic date for the whole book is too strong for this one point. The great British trio, Westcott, Hort, and Lightfoot, favored the Neronic date, but no one of the group made a special study of Revelation; we can more safely disagree with them here than elsewhere. Between 90 and 96 is probably the safest date.

We know nothing as to the dates of the Epistles. They seem to have come from about the same time as the Gospel, so they are usually dated around the nineties.

All of the Johannine literature comes from about the same general time, late in the first century. We cannot determine the order in which the books appeared.

The Fourth Gospel

Like the synoptic gospels, the Fourth Gospel tells about the life of Jesus. John very definitely tells us, though, in 20:30, 31, that he has made his selection of incidents for the purpose of proving that Jesus was the Christ, the Son of God, so that his readers might come to believe in Him and have life through Him. We have more than mere history here. But does John disregard the facts of history? It was once fashionable to disregard the Fourth Gospel in reconstructing a picture of the historical Jesus, at least in certain quarters. That is not so often done now. The real Radical disregards about as much in the synoptics as he does in John; the Conservative has no reason for disregarding either. The synoptics and John both picture a divine, miracle-working Jesus. They tell different stories from the life of Jesus, but all together they tell only a small part of the stories that might have been told; and the stories that they have in common are not contradictory, though, of course, there are problems of harmonization, just as there are problems of harmonization among the synoptics themselves. If we are right in believing that the Apostle John wrote the Gospel, we are justified in giving great credence to it as the testimony of an eye-witness. We are not at all sure that John attempts to give his incidents in chronological order; but as he gives more chronological data than the synoptists, it is customary for the harmonists to use the Johannine outline and fit the synoptic material into it in about a three-year ministry.

The Fourth Gospel was written by an old man. The author had not only known Jesus in person for some three years, but had known Him as his Lord and Master for half a century more. Jesus meant everything to him, and he wanted Jesus to come to mean everything to his readers. He chose just those incidents that had meant so much to him. He gives those events and his own interpretation of and feeling about them. John has become so filled with the spirit of Jesus that it is frequently impossible to tell where the words of Jesus stop and John's interpretation of them starts; the maker of a red-letter Testament frequently has to resort to guesses in John.

John had been living for some years in the midst of Hellenic rather than Hebraic culture. His Gospel was written to meet the needs of his time. The prologue of the Gospel asserts that Jesus was the *Logos* of the philosophers. The contemplative mood of philosophy is felt more in John than in the synoptics. Jesus Christ and His Gospel are ever the same, but they can be presented in new terms and thoughts to meet new ages and conditions.

John seems to have brought his Gospel to a close at the end of the twentieth chapter. Some think that 21 was added later by another person. It is a postscript, but the fact that the style of it is so similar to the style of the rest of the Gospel makes us feel rather strongly that John himself wrote it, we do not know how long afterwards. It may be that "and we know that his testimony is true," in verse 24, was added by some authoritative group on the margin of the manuscript and later crept into the text; though the "we" may be editorial, the verse then becoming like 19:35. Some commentators have suggested various rearrangements of the various chapters and verses of the Gospel, but the reasons advanced are far from convincing.

A brief outline of the contents of the Gospel was given in connection with the synoptic gospels in the chapter, "The Life of Christ."

First John

The Gospel was written primarily to induce persons to believe in Christ; the First Epistle was written to those who had become Christians. John tells us that he had several purposes in mind as he wrote: that those who believe might *know* that they have eternal life (5:13), that they might enjoy fellowship with other Christians (1:3), and that, therefore, their joy might be full (1:4). The aged apostle writes, as a father to his spiritual children, a very tender and practical letter. He gives many tests by which we may become sure that we are Christ's, so that we may really enjoy the benefits of salvation in this world. He warns the little children of many of the dangers of the Christian life. He gives instructions as to how they may grow in the Christian graces. By means of this little letter, the Apostle John has become the spiritual father of many generations of little children and has helped in their growth in Christ.

John writes in a most informal way, seemingly following no logical plan. Any analysis of the contents will be unsatisfactory, but the following is suggested:

I. *Introduction, 1:1-4.*
II. *The problem of sin, 1:5 - 3:12.*
III. *The duty of love, 3:13-24; 4:7-21.*
IV. *Truth and error, 4:1-6.*
V. *The tests of faith, 5:1-21.*

Second John

The First Epistle had neither the beginning nor the ending of a regular letter, but the Second and Third have both. John calls himself "The Elder" in both Epistles. Both close with a short formal salutation. The Second Epistle was written to "the elect lady and her children." Some think that that refers to some particular Christian woman and her children; if so, no one knows who she was. Some think that John used that way of speaking of some particular church and its members; if so, no one knows where the church was, except that it was probably in Asia Minor. Some think that the Greek word translated "lady" should be capitalized and read as a proper name—"To the elect Cyria and her children"; if so, we know nothing further about Cyria. Some would make the two words read "the lady Eklekte." Any one of these interpretations can be defended, but we cannot be sure which one is right.

The letter contains only one short chapter, which may be analyzed as follows:

I. *Salutation, 1-3.*
II. *Encouragement to continue in love, 4-6.*
III. *Duty of avoiding false doctrine, 7-11.*
IV. *Conclusion, 12-13.*

Third John

The Third Epistle was written by "The Elder" to "the well-beloved Gaius." There are several Gaiuses in the New Testament, but it is impossible to identify this Gaius with any other one. He was probably a rather prominent member in one of the churches of Asia Minor, but all we know about him comes from the little Epistle itself.

This, too, is a very short, personal letter of one chapter, which may be divided thus:

I. *Salutation, 1.*
II. *Thanksgiving for his walking in truth, 2-4.*
III. *Commendation of his hospitality, 5-8.*
IV. *Warning against Diotrephes, 9-11.*
V. *Commendation of Demetrius, 12.*
VI. *Conclusion, 13-14.*

Revelation

The Book of Revelation is the only book of prophecy in the New Testament, though there are certain short prophecies to be found elsewhere. Revelation belongs to a certain definite literary type, the apocalypse. There are apocalyptic elements in the Old Testament prophetical books, but Daniel is the only book in the Old Testament that we may call an apocalypse. Outside the canon of Holy Scripture, however, we have rather numerous examples of apocalypses in Jewish and Christian literature, such as the apocalypses of Enoch, Baruch, Adam, Elijah, Zephaniah, Peter, and Paul, and *The Testaments of the Twelve Patriarchs, The Book of Jubilees, The Sibylline Oracles*, and *The Psalms of Solomon.*[14] The student of Revelation should

---

[14] For examples of these see Charles, **The Apocrypha and Pseudepigrapha of the Old Testament**, and James, **The Apocryphal New Testament.**

familiarize himself with these works so that he will be in a position to evaluate the literary features used in the apocalyptic type. The Conservative believes that Revelation is inspired while the extra-canonical apocalypses are not; but they use the same literary type.

The Historical Background of Revelation

Revelation was written by John to a group of seven churches in the Roman province of Asia, in western Asia Minor. It was written in the last years of the first century, towards the end of the reign of the Roman emperor, Domitian (81-96). Some of the churches were large, some small; the cities in which the churches were located also varied in size. But they were all in the midst of a pagan Roman civilization, with all of its temptations and tribulations for Christians. Most of the Christians had come from the various pagan cults that filled the world in those days, and there was always a temptation to go back to the old ways and friends. Just at this time, however, an especially acute situation has arisen for Christianity. The Emperor Domitian allows himself to be elevated to the god-head during his lifetime and demands that he be worshipped. This Caesar-cult had been gradually growing for over a century, but the zeal of Domitian and the rulers of the Province of Asia seems to have been responsible for the development of the cult to such an extent that those who refused to worship before the image of the Emperor were persecuted. Members of other cults had no objection to worshiping the Emperor along with their own cult gods. But a Christian could not; he could have only one God. Failure to worship the Emperor brought on persecution of various sorts. Some were tortured. Some were exiled. Some were refused permission to buy or sell in the markets unless they had a pass certifying that they had bowed down and worshiped. Some were killed. The Asian Christians were suffering what the Roman Christians had suffered under Nero. There was a crisis in the church. Many were wondering if Christianity were worth all it was costing. Some were giving in to the Roman demands. All were wondering why God was allowing all these things to happen and how long He would let them go on. The Book of Revelation was written to meet this very definite crisis; there can be no true interpretation of the book which neglects this fact.

Methods of Interpretation of Revelation

Various methods of interpreting Revelation have been used down through the centuries, but we shall consider only those methods that are in rather general use at the present. Various divisions have been made, but we shall use probably the most common.

The Continuous-historical. This school of interpretation thinks of Revelation as a kind of almanac. The visions in Revelation are supposed to represent events following one after the other from some time in past history to the end of time. These students disagree widely as to the starting point, at least from Adam to Christ. Each student works the scheme out so that the end of time falls in his own time. As each new generation arises, it is necessary to work out a new scheme for the identification of events. All of the identifications are most arbitrary and fanciful. No one who studies the widely divergent conclusions reached by this school through the centuries is likely to become a member of this school and believe in the particular scheme which makes his own days necessarily the last days.

The Futurist. This school of interpreters thinks of

Revelation as being a prediction of the events of the last days. Most of the futurists think of all of Revelation after the letters to the churches as being predictive of just those events immediately preceding the Second Coming and going on down into eternity. This school tends to lose sight of the first-century Asian churches and their needs. Most members of the school have worked out quite an elaborate plan for these future events, though they do not agree among themselves as to details, much of the identification being rather arbitrary. As this is all in the future, past history cannot disprove this interpretation as it has done in the case of the earlier continuous-historical schemes.

The Preterist. This school emphasizes the historical background to such an extent that the real prophetic element is excluded. Revelation is considered a purely human message of encouragement to the churches. The visions apply to first-century events or are human guesses as to the general future. Many preterists think that the author formed his book by taking the visions from other apocalyptic books that he knew and adapting them to his purposes.

It seems to be best to take a combination of these last two schools to get a true interpretation. It is certainly necessary to remember the historical situation and interpret the book so as to make it minister to the needs of those first-century Christians; any interpretation that would be meaningless to them cannot be considered a true interpretation. But taking this view does not make it necessary to exclude the predictive element. The Conservative believes that the book must be treated as real prophecy, inspired by God. Some of the book is taken up with a divine interpretation of first-century events, events contemporaneous with, or in the near future from, the Asian Christians. But some of the book leaps down into the distant future and tells about that time when the tables will be turned, when the cause of Christ, rather than pagan Rome, will be triumphant. They are urged to live in the light of eternity. This combination method of interpretation raises difficulties, as it is sometimes impossible to tell where the dividing line is between the past and the future; but the book seems definitely to demand some such method of handling. This makes the book have a vital meaning for those persecuted early Christians; and we need only adapt the message slightly to make it vital for us today.

We must remember that the apocalypse makes use of various figures of speech. It would have meant death to have talked openly against Rome in those days, so various figures had to be used, such as Babylon, the harlot, the beast. The author could assume that his readers knew exactly the meaning of the figures and symbolism used. At times, the most careful study fails to tell us today what the meaning of a certain figure is; every wise interpreter will refrain from too much dogmatism.

Interpreters of various schools have made use of the hypothesis of *synchronism*. The various visions do not seem always to picture events that follow one another in chronological order. The same event is pictured over and over again from different angles, under different figures. At times there is chronological progress; at times, complete synchronism; at times, partial synchronism; at times, we cannot tell. Time means little in the light of eternity; remember how the prophecies of the first and second comings of Jesus were mingled with no hint that there would be at least nineteen hundred years between them.

It may be said that the Pre-, Post-, and Nonmillenarian methods of interpretation are methods held by Conservatives in their interpretation of only a part of one chapter of Revelation, the twentieth; they have nothing to do, necessarily, with the interpretation of the book as a whole. A discussion of those views belongs under an interpretation of that passage or a discussion of eschatology in systematic theology.

An Outline of Revelation

I. *Seven letters, 1:1 - 3:22.* After a short introduction, John gives a magnificent vision of the glorified Christ. The persecuted Christians of Asia Minor are reminded of the glories of their Lord, Who is far more glorious than even the Roman Emperor. Remember that He is with you, no matter who may be against you. This glorified Christ knows what is going on in the various churches, and He sends to each one a letter, telling the real condition of the church and warning of certain dangers, commending certain good features, telling the punishment that is in store for those who fail and the glorious rewards that are in store for those who remain true. Prepare for persecution by looking up to the glorified Christ, and by looking within, to weed out the bad and strengthen the good.

II. *Seven seals, 4:1 - 8:1.* As an introduction to this section, John presents a vision of God on His throne. He lives; He rules; all that happens, happens in accordance with His will. Then the Lamb takes a roll of destiny and opens, one by one, its seven seals. The first four seals bring forth four riders on colored horses, representing, probably, triumphant militarism, bloodshed, famine, and death. Those Asian Christians knew well that that was a correct picture of the conditions under which they were living under Rome. With little adaptation, that is a picture of the conditions under which Christians are still living. At the opening of the fifth seal, the scene changes to heaven, and we see beneath the altar the souls of those who had died for their faith. They are still interested in the conditions on earth, and they ask God how long He is going to allow the good to suffer and the evil to triumph. They are told that the present condition must last some longer until all the elect have been gathered in; in God's own good time things will be made right. At the sixth seal, we are taken down into the last days and see the calamities that are to accompany the end of the world and the punishment that God is going to send upon the ungodly. Then there is a little interlude in which we see that God is going to protect those that are His from all the calamities, and we see a little foretaste of the glories that will be theirs. The seventh seal brings a half-hour's silence, allowing the reader to imagine the glories of eternity, or serving as an introduction to the next great action.

III. *Seven trumpets, 8:2 - 11:19.* After a short introduction, seven trumpeters sound their trumpets, one by one. The trumpets go more into detail in working out the punishment that God is sending and will send upon the ungodly world. The first four trumpets give terrible pictures of the wrath of God as it affects nature, the earth, the sea, the rivers, and the heavenly bodies. The fifth and sixth give vivid pictures of the punishment sent on men themselves. Then again we have an interlude, giving several short visions, emphasizing again the fact that God will preserve those who are His. The seventh trumpet brings in the establishment of the eternal kingdom of God.

IV. *Miscellaneous visions, 12:1 - 14:20.* The woman, probably the Church, bears a manchild, Christ. The Dragon, Satan, is waiting to kill Him at His birth. He is taken up into heaven. Satan goes up to try to kill Him there. Satan is thrown out of heaven to the earth. Satan then tries to destroy the woman, the Church.

Again he is unsuccessful. To the aid of the Dragon come two Beasts, probably representing the Roman Empire and the Roman Religion, especially emperor worship. So the anti-Christian trinity is completed.

But we see other pictures. A great host of the elect is on Mount Zion. These and the angels sing their songs of praise to God.

Then again we go down to the end of the world and see it pictured under the common figure of a harvest.

V. *Seven bowls, 15:1 - 16:21.* After an introduction, seven angels pour out the contents of their seven bowls, one by one. The bowls have similarities with the trumpets and with the Egyptian plagues. They present more terrible pictures of the wrath of God against the ungodly world, leading up again to the end of the world and the final conflict between good and evil.

VI. *Miscellaneous visions, 17:1 - 22:21.* The fall of the mighty city of Babylon is described in the most vivid detail. Rome, and all wicked cities like Rome and old Babylon, will receive their just dues.

The Royal Warrior, Christ, comes and overthrows the two Beasts and consigns them to eternal torment. Rome and her religion—wicked states and false religions of all time—receive their rewards.

Satan himself is overcome by Christ and sent finally to hell.

The book reaches its glorious climax with a wonderful word picture of heaven. Those who are faithful to Christ may incur persecution on earth, but they will enjoy eternal bliss in heaven. But the ungodly will have no part in heaven.

Then there is a concluding section, warning against making any changes in the book, urging Christians to remain faithful, and praying for the coming again of our Lord.

APPENDIX
AND
INDEX

APPENDIX I

New Testament Chronology

(Dates are approximate. See appropriate sections for discussions.)

6 B.C.	Birth of Jesus
26 A.D.	Beginning of Ministry of John
27	Beginning of Ministry of Jesus
30	Crucifixion of Jesus
33	Conversion of Paul
35	Paul's Famine Visit to Jerusalem
45	Epistle of James
46-48	First Missionary Journey
48	Jerusalem Council
48	Galatians
49-52	Second Missionary Journey
50	Gospel of Mark
50	First and Second Thessalonians
51	Gallio Becomes Proconsul at Corinth
52-56	Third Missionary Journey
55	First Corinthians
56	Second Corinthians
56	Romans
56-58	Paul in Jerusalem and Caesarea
59-61	Paul's First Roman Imprisonment

59	Ephesians, Colossians, and Philemon
60	Gospels of Matthew and Luke
61	Philippians
61	Acts
62	First Timothy and Titus
64	First Peter
65	Hebrews
67	Second Peter and Jude
67	Second Timothy
67	Martyrdom of Paul and Peter
95	The Johannine Literature

Appendix II

THE MIRACULOUS IN THE NEW TESTAMENT

The miraculous is the great storm center in the controversy between the Conservative and the Liberal or Radical views of Christianity. The Bible is so full of the miraculous element that if a person cannot believe in the miraculous, it will be impossible for him to hold any theory of the inspiration and authority of the Bible that is at all compatible with the Conservative view of religion. We cannot attempt a complete discussion of the miraculous here; we shall review rather briefly some of the attempts that have been made to eject the miracles from the New Testament, criticise these attempts, and try to show that it is still possible for a person in the twentieth century to believe in the miraculous in the light of all the facts that can be presented by natural science and Biblical scholarship.

The first point that we wish to make is, that natural science does not disprove miracles.

Through the ages, natural science has been gradually reducing nature to order. A regularity has been observed. By noticing and using these natural laws, science has been able to make the remarkable progress that has meant so much to the civilization of the world, especially in the last hundred years. Every one of us must join in singing the praises of science in the highest terms; nothing that we shall say should be construed as in any way casting aspersions upon the scientific quest of the truth that has been making us free and that will continue to make us even more free as we discover more and more of it.

It was only natural, however, that some — even many — scientists should come to think too highly of their generalizations. Darwin discovered many facts that have been useful to science. He made certain generalizations that have also been valuable. But he thought so highly of his scientific theories that he elevated them to the undue rank of a philosophy to explain the universe. Everything could be explained by his theory of evolution. Of course, he could not explain it all, but he felt that science could in time, on the basis of his theory. Darwin wanted his theory to take even the place of God.

Of course, such an atheistic and materialistic theory makes miracles impossible. But do the facts in the case make it necessary to hold such a theory? By no means. Theories of evolution are still in good repute in scientific quarters, but there is nothing in evolution that is inherently atheistic or materialistic. Many of the best scientists believe in a theistic evolution now, which has a place for God as the creator and guide of the universe. There is nothing in a theistic view of evolution that would make the miraculous impossible. Then, too, we must remember that theories of evolution in all their various forms are still theories, not facts.

We must not make the mistake of supposing that natural science can prove the miraculous for us. Miracles are not every-day occurrences; they cannot be examined in test tubes or under microscopes. We can affirm confidently, though, that there are no facts of natural science that make it impossible to believe in miracles. Certain scientists still hold theories and philosophies that have no place for the miraculous, but these are just theories and philosophies; and they are not the only theories and philosophies that can rationally be held by scientific men in the light of all the twentieth century knowledge. Many scientists believe that natural science leaves a place for miracles, and that historical science then proves that miracles have actually occurred.

The next point that we wish to make is, that Biblical scholarship has failed to disprove the miraculous. It may sound strange to some that we should state this point in such a fashion. But Biblical scholars have sought in various ways to expunge the miraculous from the Bible. At times, this was done with the very best of motives. Various theories were put forward trying to make it possible for a man to believe in his religion and science at the same time, at a time when most scientists had no place for miracles in their scheme of things. Science and religion could never harmonize on an atheistic basis, but various attempts were made, and are still being made, to harmonize on a deistic basis. Let there be a God to get things started; but after that, God can do nothing new; there must be no miracles. So we have the development of a class of Biblical scholars who, more or less consciously, start with an absolute rule of criticism like Renan's and deny a place in history to any miraculous narrative. But the Bible is full of miracles; what shall be done?

First, an attempt was made to naturalize the miracles and thus explain them away. They said: "The Bible writers thought that certain events were miracles, but we can see today that they were just strange events that can be explained on a purely naturalistic basis." This method was very popular in certain circles, especially throughout the nineteenth century. Schweitzer's classic book, *The Quest of the Historical Jesus,* gives a full treatment. We shall give only a few examples.

When Jesus is reported to have worked a miracle of healing, He really worked no miracle, but worked through His spiritual power on the nervous system, or He used some medicines known to Him alone. Evil spirits were cast out, at least partly, by the use of sedatives.

Jesus did not really walk on the water, but as He was walking on the shore in the mist, the disciples thought He was walking on the water. The sea was not miraculously calmed, but the boat simply rounded a headland and got out of the storm center.

Jesus did not have to work a miracle to feed the multitude. All the people had their lunches, but each one was afraid to start eating, lest there should not be enough for himself and those with whom he would have to share. Jesus pulled out His lunch and set the good example of starting to share. Soon all the lunches were out; there was more than enough.

The supposed raisings from the dead were considered simply deliverances from premature burial; the "dead" had simply swooned. Even Jesus had simply swooned on the cross; the cool grave and the spices served to resuscitate Him; the storm and earthquake completed the job and also rolled the stone from the mouth of the tomb.

Bahrdt and Venturini made Jesus the tool of a secret society of Essenes, who wanted to gain strength for their society by staging seemingly miraculous performances. A mysterious Persian gives Jesus two sovereign remedies, one for affections of the eye, the other for nervous disorders. Through Haram, a prominent member of the order, Luke the physician is supposed to have been introduced to Jesus and placed all his science at His disposal. The feeding of the multitude is carefully prepared for. A cave is filled with provisions by the society. At the proper time, Jesus backs up to the mouth of the cave, and the food is passed out to Him. Aided by the flowing oriental robes, it is a simple sleight-of-hand trick. The walking on the water is easily accomplished by simply tying a raft to the back of the boat.

The supreme miracle to be staged by the Society was a resurrection of the dead. The Society gets Jesus crucified. Jesus utters a loud cry and feigns death. Nicodemus has Him taken down immediately, and he and Dr. Luke are able to resuscitate Him.

Such are some of the typical naturalizations; some are fairly plausible; others are utterly absurd. Schweitzer laughs this whole method out of court. He points out, also, that the New Testament authors, on this basis, can save their own honesty and sincerity only at the expense of the sincerity of their characters; they make the disciples of Jesus see miracles where they could not possibly have seen them; and make Jesus Himself allow miracles to be imagined where He must necessarily have protested against such a delusion. Since the publication of Schweitzer's book, the method of naturalizing away the miracles has practically passed out of fashion among Biblical scholars. About the only place where that method is now used is in the magazine sections of some of the more sensational Sunday newspapers.

Another great method of ridding the Bible of miracles is the developmental or source theory. We all admit that there is a tendency to make the lives of great men more and more wonderful the further we get from the actual lives of the men. For example, Xavier mentions no miracles in his own letters, but the further we get from his own lifetime, the more miracles we find attributed to him. The theory is that we can see the same development in the different strata of documents in the Bible. Let us go back, then, to the earliest documents where we find the fewest miracles, and then assume that if we could get back to the actual events themselves we would find no miracles at all.

The theory sounds most reasonable, but what are the facts? Probably the earliest literature of certain date is the Pauline Epistles. They do not mention many miracles, because Paul was not writing historical documents; but Paul does recognize miracles, and he makes one of the greatest of them, the resurrection of Jesus, one of the central points and strongest proofs of his gospel—"If Christ be not risen, then is our preaching vain, and your faith is also vain," I Cor. 15: 14. And Paul gives as proof that Jesus did rise the list of eye-witnesses, many of whom were still alive when Paul wrote this letter.

When we turn to the gospels, all scholars agree that Mark is the earliest, followed by Matthew and Luke, and finally by John. It is true that we find details about certain miracles in Matthew and Luke that are not in the earlier gospel, Mark. We would think it strange if this were not true when we remember that Mark is only about half as long as Matthew or Luke or John. And is it not rather strange, on this developmental theory, that we find in the earliest, shortest gospel, Mark, twenty miracles; while in the later and much longer gospels, Matthew and Luke, we find just twenty-two and twenty-one; and in the latest gospel of all, John, we find only eight?[1] And the early, Markan, list includes all classes of miracles, even the raising from the dead in the case of Jairus' daughter.

We find the miracles in the very earliest strata in the New Testament writings. And we may add that the same is true if we analyze the gospels into their sources. The source "Q" used by Matthew and Luke was as early as Mark, or even earlier. The document contains fewer than three hundred verses, and most of it is discourse material. Yet in this short, early document, composed largely of sayings of Jesus, we have,

---

[1] Croscup, **Historical Charts of the Life and Ministry of Christ**, p. 30.

according to Streeter's reconstruction[2], the account of the temptation of Jesus, which was probably meant to be taken with supernatural intent[3], the healing of the centurion's servant at a distance,[4] the casting out of a dumb demon,[5] and the command: "Go your way, and tell John what things ye have seen and heard; how that the blind see, the lame walk, the lepers are cleansed, the deaf hear, and the dead are raised." [6]

We see, then, that Mark is full of the miraculous, containing even more in proportion than any of the later gospels. The other best-known source, "Q," has a rather surprisingly large miraculous element. Then, of course, the separate infancy sources for Matthew and Luke contain the virgin birth, and the passion and resurrection sources contain the resurrection, to say nothing of the other miraculous events. We can find no written source for the life of Jesus which does not contain miracles.

When we go back of the written sources, we are on very intangible and uncertain ground. The *formgeschichte* scholars in recent years have made attempts to reconstruct the growth of the oral tradition back of all the written sources. There is entirely too much indefiniteness as yet for us to give much credence to their reconstructions, but it is interesting to note, however, that most of these scholars make the earliest form of the oral tradition the Christian preaching. The center of this preaching is that Jesus was the Messiah of Old Testament prophecy, that He died for the salvation of those that would believe on Him, and that He was raised again from the dead.

Go back, then, to our earliest sources, and we find

---

[2] **The Four Gospels,** p. 291.
[3] Mt. 4:1-11, Lk. 4:1-13.
[4] Mt. 8:5-13, Lk. 7:1-10.
[5] Mt. 9:32-33, Lk. 11:14.
[6] Mt. 11:4-5, Lk. 7:22.

the miraculous. The developmental theory will not explain away the miracles; at times it seems to work beautifully the wrong way.

Another way that some Biblical scholars try to get rid of the miracles is by what we may call the superstitious age theory. Although our earliest sources contain miracles, yet, it is said, all those sources come from an age when people were credulous and superstitious. Just as we do not believe the ghost stories of our negro servants, so we should not be expected to believe the miracle stories of those superstitious people of the first century. Of course, we may readily admit that people did not have the same ideas about the regularity of nature then that we have now. We may also admit that there were many superstitious people then. But one cannot afford to be too dogmatic about generalizations, about saying that people as a whole were credulous. There are plenty of superstitions and superstitious people in the twentieth century. Think of the dream books, the ghost stories, the various superstitions that are found so frequently among the black people but which are not limited to them by any means. Think of the astrologers and fortune tellers that you hear over the radio. Think of great ocean liners delaying their sailing hour until after Friday the thirteenth. And so we could go on. We cannot prove that everyone in the twentieth century is superstitious; neither can anyone prove that all were superstitious in the first century. Specifically, we cannot prove that the writers of the New Testament were superstitious, unless, of course, we define a superstitious person as anyone who believes in a miracle, which would be simply arguing in a circle. This whole theory is open to fewest objections because it is so intangible; and yet, for the same reason, it can be less dogmatic about its claims to have explained away the miracles.

We have seen that there are no facts of modern natural science which disprove miracles. Certain theories and philosophies which are held by some scientific men have no place for the miraculous, but those are not the only theories and philosophies that can be held. If your scientific theories will not allow you to believe in miracles, then you must explain them away. The attempts of the naturalizing scholars have proved failures. Tracing the development from the earliest sources fails to eliminate the miracles. So the best thing that you can do is to say that you just will not believe the sources because they come from an age when you think people were credulous and superstitious. And many honest, thoughtful, reverent people are taking that position today.

But, on the other hand, if your scientific theories and your philosophies allow you to have a place for miracles, then you are in a position to examine the historical evidence in favor of the miracles. Our earliest sources are full of the miraculous. These sources have the ear-marks of credibility; they were written by honest men who were in a position to know the facts; several of the sources can, on good critical grounds, be traced back to eye-witnesses. These men believed their testimony to such an extent that they were willing to live and die for it. The Christian Church is here, and its beginning must be explained. Paul said that there would have been no Christianity but for the miracle of the resurrection of Jesus; something certainly happened to change the despair of Calvary to the triumph of Pentecost. Historic Christianity was founded on miracles; it has lived through the centuries with its belief in miracles. Historical science will prove the miraculous in the New Testament to anyone whose theories of science and philosophy allow him to weigh the evidence without bias.

If, then, after having weighed all the evidence carefully and critically, you come to a belief that the miracle stories of the New Testament are true, you will be in a position to believe in the historicity of the New Testament, and, in turn, to believe in a high doctrine of the inspiration of the Scriptures, and to believe in Christianity as a supernaturally revealed religion.

Appendix III

THE INSPIRATION OF THE BIBLE

II Timothy 3: 16, 17 says, "All scripture is given by inspiration of God, and is profitable for doctrine, for reproof, for correction, for instruction in righteousness; that the man of God may be perfect, thoroughly furnished unto all good works." The words "given by inspiration of God" are one compound word in the Greek, meaning "God-breathed."

These words in II Timothy give us a general statement of the Conservative belief about the Bible. The Conservative believes that the Bible is God's Word; he takes his religion from it as a divine, authoritative revelation. He believes that the Bible is the only God-breathed book; Biblical inspiration should be clearly distinguished from the inspiration of Shakespeare, for example.

The Proofs of Inspiration

One of the classic statements of the proofs of the inspiration of the Bible is contained in the Westminster Confession of Faith, chapter I, section V: "We may be moved and induced by the testimony of the Church to an high and reverent esteem for the Holy Scripture; and the heavenliness of the matter, the efficacy of the doctrine, the majesty of the style, the consent of all the parts, the scope of the whole (which is to give all glory to God), the full discovery it makes of the only way of man's salvation, the many other incomparable excellencies, and the entire perfection thereof, are arguments whereby it doth abundantly evidence itself to be the Word of God; yet, notwithstanding, our full persuasion and assurance of the infallible truth, and divine authority thereof, is from the inward work of the Holy Spirit, bearing witness by and with the Word in our hearts." Every phrase is worthy of careful consideration; let us look briefly at a few of them.

"The testimony of the Church . . . " The true Church through all the ages has believed in the inspiration of the Bible and has used the Bible as its source of belief. We are in the company of the saints through the ages when we hold that belief.

"The efficacy of the doctrine . . . the full discovery it makes of the only way of man's salvation . . ." Man is lost in sin; he needs salvation, reconciliation to God. The Bible shows man how he may be saved, how he may be born again unto God and how he may live as a child of God. The Bible claims to do this, and countless Christians can say that they know that the Bible's claims are true because they have actually worked in their own lives.

"The consent of all the parts . . ." The Bible was written by many human authors over a period of some sixteen hundred years, yet the different parts harmonize in a wonderful way; all of them play their parts in the preparation for, and the application of, the salvation wrought by Christ. Back of all the human writers must have been a divine Editor; otherwise we should have expected confusion and contradiction.

"The heavenliness of the matter . . . the majesty of the style . . . the many other incomparable excellencies, and the entire perfection thereof . . ." The Bible has the marks of heaven upon it; it looks like more than a human book.

"Our full persuasion and assurance of the infallible truth, and divine authority thereof, is from the inward work of the Holy Spirit, bearing witness by and with the Word in our hearts." This is the final proof for the Conservative. He realizes that these other proofs, and others that could be adduced, do not furnish absolute logical proof that God is the author of Scripture; they point very strongly to that conclusion, but they do not furnish an incontrovertible demonstration. The Conservative *knows* that the Bible is God's Word because the Holy Spirit bears that witness in his heart. That is a mystical thing, but it is a very real thing. The love of a mother for her child is probably not capable of logical or scientific proof; it is another example of a very real mystical thing.

The Method of Inspiration

How did God inspire the Bible, make it His own Word? He worked through human authors. As Jesus was the God-man, so the Bible is a divine-human book.

Some Conservatives have held to a mechanical, dictation theory of inspiration—that every word was dictated by God, that the writers of Scripture were mere pens in the hand of God. Of course, God could have worked that way, but the facts of Scripture seem to prove conclusively that He did not work that way.

Most Conservatives hold to a dynamic theory of inspiration. God treated the human authors as real men. We see their different personalities in their writings. Luke-Acts is the highly polished work of a master of style; Mark is quite rough and rugged. Paul's letters show us the mind of the brilliant, though impetuous, thinker. God did not take away the humanity of the authors of Scripture; He worked back of it. God guided and superintended them as they worked, so that the books of Scripture which they produced were perfect for producing the results that He desired.

At times the Scripture writers did get their material by direct revelation from God, as in the case of some of the prophetical writings. When a miracle is necessary, God can work one.

For the most part, however, the writers got their material in more normal ways. At times they simply wrote what they had seen with their own eyes and heard with their own ears. At times they got their information from others who had seen and heard, as Mark probably got his information from Peter for most of his gospel. At times they made use of written sources, as Matthew and Luke almost certainly did. God wanted them to make use of their minds and the human sources available.

Back of the human activity was the divine superintendence. The Holy Spirit saw that they used the right sources and used them in the right way, that the writings they produced were the kind of writings that He wanted them to be.

THE GUARANTEES OF INSPIRATION

What kinds of writings did God want them to be? How far does inspiration guarantee the truth of the Scriptures?

II Timothy says that the inspired Scriptures are "profitable for doctrine, for reproof, for correction, for instruction in righteousness: that the man of God may be perfect, thoroughly furnished unto all good works." The Westminster Shorter Catechism says: "The Scriptures principally teach what man is to believe concerning God and what duty God requires of man."

All Conservatives believe that the Bible is our authority in matters of religion. It is our infallible rule of faith and practice. Our religious beliefs come from the Bible. We seek no other way of salvation than that taught in Scripture. We are content to order our lives by the principles of what we believe to be the final code of ethics taught therein. We test our creeds and our lives by a divine authority that will never fail.

While the Bible is primarily a book of religion, it also has history and science and other things in it. How far does inspiration guarantee the truth of these other things? Here Conservatives are not in complete agreement, and many of them are quite frankly looking for more light before reaching dogmatic conclusions.

We shall certainly expect the history and science to be accurate when they are teaching religious truths that may be harmed by inaccuracy. There are times, however, when the historical and scientific matters are purely incidental, and it would make no religious difference in the world whether thirty-two or thirty-three thousand men were killed in a certain battle. Are the historical and scientific matters accurate when they make no religious difference? Frequently we may be sure that they are; time and again they have been proved accurate. But are they always accurate in every detail?

Many Conservatives believe in verbal inerrancy. They may be entirely correct, though many Conservatives do not believe in it. All Conservatives should realize that a belief in verbal inerrancy is not essential to a high view of inspiration. We should all keep in mind certain facts such as the following:

The words that we have in Scripture are not inerrant in the sense that they are grammatically perfect. One with only a slight acquaintance with Greek can see that Revelation has many constructions that violate the fundamental rules of grammar, for example. But although the grammar is sometimes bad, that fact does not hurt the religious teaching of the book in the least.

When we have parallel accounts, there are often verbal differences. We have the inscription on the cross in all four gospels, and each time it is different. The words are different, but the important thing is that the sense is the same. Many of the sayings of Jesus occur in several gospels, and the same verbal differences occur. We may wish that we had the very words that our Lord spoke, but the fact is that we can be sure only of the correct sense.

There are places where Scripture seems to contradict itself. There are some very difficult problems of harmonization. Before admitting a contradiction, though, we must be sure that we have the correct text of the passages under consideration and that our interpretation of each is correct.

There are places where Scripture seems to contradict facts of history and science. Again, we must be sure of the text and the interpretation of the passage. And we must be sure of the fact of history or science. It is quite fashionable in certain quarters to find contradictions between Scripture and Josephus, say, and assume immediately that Josephus is right and Scripture wrong; the Conservative thinks that it is just as fair to think that Scripture may be right and Josephus wrong. We must carefully distinguish between fact and theory in the realm of science. Scripture, of course, cannot harmonize with every scientific theory; there are frequently contradictory theories. Unwise interpretations of the Bible have caused much trouble between science and religion. Conservatives today do not think that they must believe in witches or a flat earth to believe in the Bible, though men have so believed. Some Conservatives believe in creation in seven days of twenty-four hours; many feel that that is not a necessary interpretation of Genesis. It is regrettable that there has been so much warfare between theologians and scientists; both sides have things of which they may well be ashamed. We are all human. But let us all together search for more truth, and let us be willing to follow the facts wherever they may lead us.

All of the apparent contradictions between Scripture and history and science have not yet been solved. It may be that there are no contradictions; many Conservatives believe this. Others believe that there are, or may be, contradictions in matters such as history or science, but not such as will affect the religious teaching of Scripture. Normally Scripture is very accurate in matters of history. Historical science and archaeology have time and again proved the accuracy of Scripture in places where it had been denied. And although no one is in position to know the complete facts of creation, it is remarkable that the early chapters of Genesis, written so long ago, have so much in common with the best scientific thought today.

The Conservative believes that inspiration guarantees the infallible accuracy of the Scriptures in matters of faith and practice. He has a high respect for Biblical accuracy in all realms. Some Conservatives believe in verbal inerrancy; others are not sure. All Conservatives should realize that we must not sit back in our easy chairs and decide what we should like the Bible to be and then twist the Bible to suit that theory, but that we must hold our theories in the light of the facts of the Bible itself—and of all facts.

Some Conservatives use the terms "plenary" and "verbal" in connection with inspiration. They are good words when they are correctly understood, but they lend themselves to much misunderstanding. Neither one should be confused with inerrancy. Plenary inspiration means that the whole Bible is the Word of God; this view is in opposition to the one that holds that some of the Bible is God's Word, that the Bible contains, but is not, the Word of God. Verbal inspiration means that the words of Scripture are accurate for producing the results desired by the Holy Spirit; it does not mean that the words are perfect in every respect, necessarily, or that the words used were the only ones that could have been used. Most Conservatives believe in plenary, verbal inspiration, but many hesitate to use the terms because they are so frequently misunderstood.

The original writings in the original languages made up the inspired Bible. Of course, we no longer have the original manuscripts; but the Conservative uses the facts of textual criticism to show him how accurate his text is today and to show him where he must be in doubt as to the true reading. Many cannot use the original language; that is a great handicap to accurate interpretation, but many good translations give the sense quite accurately for all ordinary purposes.

Conservatives, quite rightly, treasure highly their belief in the inspiration of the Bible; it is one of their most distinctive beliefs. It can and should be held intelligently. It can and should be held in the light of all the facts of textual and historical criticism, in the light of all the facts that may be assembled from all quarters.

In spite of the attacks of its enemies through the centuries, in spite of the many unwise positions taken by its friends, the Bible lives on. It brings life eternal to all who hear and heed its message.

Appendix IV

BIBLIOGRAPHY

Introductions:

Dibelius, M., **Fresh Approach to the N. T. and Early Christian Literature**, Scribners, 1936.
Goodspeed, E. J., **Introduction to the N. T.**, U. of Chicago, 1937.
M'Neile, A. H., **Introduction to the N. T.**, Oxford, 1927.
Moffatt, J., **Introduction to the Literature of the N. T.**, Scribners, 1911.
Zahn, T., **Introduction to the N. T.**, 3 vol., Scribners, 1909.

Canon and Textual Criticism:

Gregory, C. R., **Canon and Text of the N. T.**, Scribners, 1907.
Kenyon, F. G., **Textual Criticism of the N. T.**, Macmillan, 1912.
Kenyon, F. G., **Text of the Greek Bible**, Duckworth, 1937.
Westcott, B. F., **Canon of the N. T.**, Macmillan, 1855.

Greek Testaments:

Nestle, E., **Novum Testamentum Graece**, Stuttgart, 16th ed.,1936
Souter, A., **Novum Testamentum Graece**, Oxford, 1910.
Westcott, B. F., and Hort, F. J. A., **New Testament in the Original Greek**, Macmillan, 1881.

N. T. Greek Grammars:

Dana, H. E., and Mantey, J. R., **Manual Grammar of the Greek N. T.**, Macmillan, 1928.
Robertson, A. T., **Grammar of the Greek N. T. in the Light of Historical Research**, Doran, 4th ed., 1923.
Robertson, A. T., and Davis, W. H., **New Short Grammar of the Greek N. T.**, R. R. Smith, 1931.

N. T. Greek Lexicons:

Liddell, H. G., and Scott, R., **Greek-English Lexicon**, new, large edition, also smaller editions, Oxford.
Souter, A., **Pocket Lexicon to the Greek N. T.**, Oxford, 1916.
Thayer, J. H., **Greek-English Lexicon of the N. T.**, American, 1886.

Bible Dictionaries and Encyclopedias:

Davis, J. D., **Dictionary of the Bible**, Doran, 4th ed., 1924.
Hastings, J., ed., **Dictionary of the Bible**, 5 vol., Scribners, 1898.
Orr, J., ed., **International Standard Bible Encyclopedia**, 5 vol., Howard-Severance, 1915.

Backgrounds:

Angus, S., **Environment of Early Christianity**, Scribners, 1914.
Mathews, S., **N. T. Times in Palestine**, New Revised ed., 1933, Macmillan.
Purves, G. T., **The Apostolic Age**, Scribners, 1900.
Smith, G. A., **Historical Geography of the Holy Land**, 20th ed., Doran, 1919.

Commentaries:

Cambridge Bible for Schools and Colleges, various authors, usually a volume to a book, Cambridge.
Cambridge Greek Testament, various authors, usually a volume to a book, Cambridge.
Erdman, C. R., **Commentaries on N. T. Books**, usually a volume to a book, Westminster.
Expositor's Greek Testament, various authors, 5 vol., Eerdmans.
International Critical Commentary, various authors, usually a volume to a book, Scribners.
Macmillan's Commentaries, various authors, usually a volume to a book.
Moffatt N. T. Commentaries, various authors, usually a volume to a book, Harpers.
Robertson, A. T., **Word Pictures in the N. T.**, 6 vol., Harpers, 1933.

INDEX

Printed in United States of America

DATE DUE

DE 22

MAR 14

DE 7

NOV 2

MAR 13

AUG 2

JAN 25

JAN 4

JUL 1

JUN 21

FEB 15

OCT 4

OCT 1

OCT 11

OCT 22

FEB 20

MAR 20

OCT 20

FEB 28